You & Wii™

Everything You Need to Know

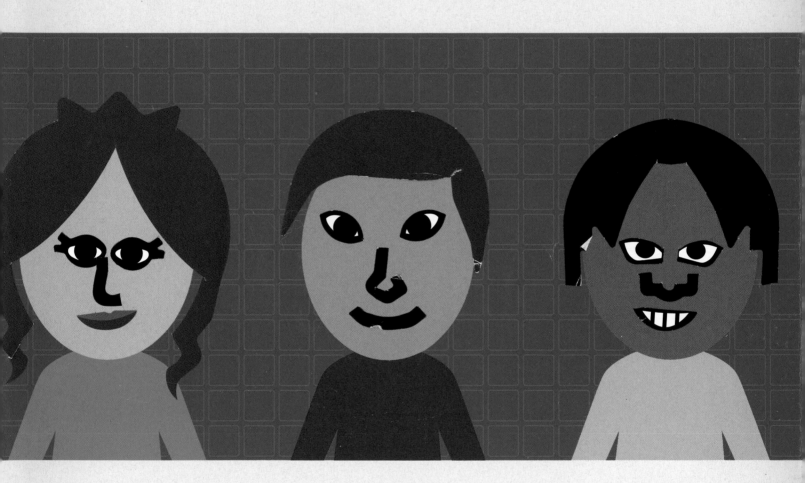

Dan Birlew

Prima Games
A Division of Random House, Inc.

3000 Lava Ridge Court
Roseville, CA 95661
(800) 733-3000

You and Wii™

PRIMA OFFICIAL GAME GUIDE

WRITTEN BY DAN BIRLEW

Prima Games
A Division of Random House, Inc.
3000 Lava Ridge Court, Suite 100
Roseville, CA 95661

www.primagames.com

Product Manager: Mario De Govia
Editor: Rebecca Chastain
Manufacturing: Suzanne Goodwin
Design: Winter Graphics North

ISBN: 978-0-7615-5575-9
Library of Congress Catalog Card Number: 2006938873
Printed in the United States of America

07 08 09 10 LL 10 9 8 7 6 5 4 3 2 1

DAN BIRLEW

Dan Birlew is the author of more than 50 official strategy guides for videogames, including titles such as *Tom Clancy's Splinter Cell: Double Agent, Naruto: Uzumaki Chronicles,* and *Reservoir Dogs The Game.* He is a graduate of the University of Texas at Austin and an ardent supporter of all its athletic programs, come rain or shine. He currently resides in Southern Nevada with his wife of thirteen years, Laura.

We want to hear from you! E-mail comments and feedback to dbirlew@primagames.com.

ACKNOWLEDGEMENTS

Completion of this book could not have been possible without the cooperation and assistance of the follow individuals: Thanks to Seth McMahill and Damon Baker and Nintendo of America, who played excellent hosts on my two trips there. More thanks to Damon Baker for providing feedback and ideas for this book. Thanks to David Hodgson and Steve Stratton, for being excellent multiplayer partners and spontaneous photography models. Thanks to David Hodgson, Eric Mylonas, and Richard Leadbetter for getting me up and going on the HD capture system used to take the screens in this book. Thanks to cvxfreak and MiamiWesker for populating my Wii with Miis resembling Resident Evil characters. Thanks to Mario De Govia and Rebecca Chastain for their hard work on this title. And special thanks to Laura, my wife, for making an excellent Mii and being a good sport.

QUICK REFERENCE

3

LEGAL

You and Wii™

QUICK REFERENCE

CONTENTS

4

CONTENTS

QUICK REFERENCE

5

CONTENTS

Welcome to Wii

[INTRODUCTION]

THE WII CONSOLE IS THE NEWEST VIDEO GAME AND MULTIMEDIA ENTERTAINMENT SYSTEM PRODUCED BY THE NINTENDO CORPORATION. THE WII IS NOT JUST FOR KIDS AND NOT JUST FOR GAMERS. WITH ITS COMPACT DESIGN, MULTIMEDIA FUNCTIONS, MESSAGE BOARD SYSTEM, AND WIRELESS INTERNET CONNECTIVITY, THE WII IS A MULTI-FUNCTIONAL SYSTEM THAT THE WHOLE FAMILY CAN USE TO SHARE MESSAGES, PHOTOS, AND VIDEOS. AND THAT'S NOT TO MENTION THAT THE SYSTEM PLAYS THE LATEST AND GREATEST NINTENDO AND THIRD-PARTY GAMES!

PROBABLY THE MOST REMARKABLE FEATURE OF THE WII IS THE WII REMOTE CONTROLLER, WHICH FEATURES ALL-NEW MOTION SENSITIVE TECHNOLOGY THAT ALLOWS YOU TO INTERACT WITH GAMES IN A WHOLE NEW WAY; NOT JUST BY PRESSING THE BUTTON, BUT BY MOVING THE CONTROLLER THROUGH SPACE TO INTERACT WITH VIRTUAL WORLDS!

THE WII PLAYS NOT ONLY BRAND-NEW WII GAMES, BUT ALSO THE ENTIRE LIBRARY OF GAMECUBE GAMES. AND WITH AN INTERNET CONNECTION, USERS CAN DOWNLOAD MANY GAMES FROM NINTENDO'S BACK LIBRARY, INCLUDING GAMES RELEASED ON THE NINTENDO ENTERTAINMENT SYSTEM (NES), SUPER NINTENDO ENTERTAINMENT SYSTEM (SNES), AND NINTENDO 64 (N64), AS WELL AS THE SEGA GENESIS AND NEC TURBOGRAFX PLATFORMS.

THE WII OPENS UP A WHOLE WORLD OF ENTERTAINMENT LIKE NO OTHER SYSTEM BEFORE IT. THIS SECTION OF THE BOOK EXPLORES EVERY FUNCTION OF THE WII CONSOLE, FROM PROPER SETUP AND CABLE CONNECTION TO MENU INTERFACES AND LOADING MEDIA. SO IF YOU'RE A VETERAN VIDEO-GAME PLAYER OR SOMEONE WHO'S NEVER USED A GAME CONSOLE BEFORE, THIS CHAPTER WILL LET YOU SET UP AND START UP WITH CONFIDENCE. NO OTHER SOURCE HELPS YOU UNDERSTAND THE WII AS CLEARLY OR COMPLETELY!

[DISC CHANNEL]

The first channel displayed at the top left corner of the Wii menu is the Disc Channel. This channel displays the title screen of any Wii or GameCube disc inserted into the Wii console unit. To begin playing the game, point the Wii Remote at Disc Channel and press Ⓐ to zoom in. Then point at the "Start" button in the channel screen's lower-right corner and press Ⓐ to initialize the game. Games sometimes need a minute or two to load, especially if the game is old or the disc needs to be cleaned.

[TIP]

When viewing a channel, press ⊖ or ⊕ to cycle through the available channels. You can also move the hand cursor to the blue arrows at either side of the screen. When the hand cursor touches an arrow, it becomes a button you can press to advance to the previous screen or the next screen, respectively from left to right.

7

[MII CHANNEL]

Mii Channel allows you to create miniature characters called "Mii"s. By changing hair and facial features in a variety of ways, you can create Mii characters that look like you, your friends and family members, or even famous persons you might have seen on television or at the movies. Mii characters saved to your system can be used as characters in certain games, such as *Wii Sports*.

Point the Wii Remote at the "Start" button in the lower-right corner of the Mii Channel screen and press Ⓐ to continue. If no Mii characters are stored on your system, or if Mii Channel is starting for the first time, then the program goes directly into the New Mii creation screen. If Mii characters are stored on your system, then the program enters a large room called "Mii Plaza," where Mii characters stored on your console mingle.

NEW MII CREATION

The first step to entering the Mii universe is to create a Mii! First, choose whether to create a male or female character. Then choose either to start a Mii character from scratch or to start with a Mii who looks similar to the character you want to create:

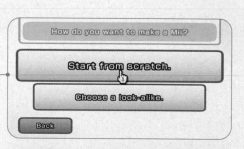

Start from scratch: Loads the "default" Mii. You may then change the appearance and settings of the Mii until you are satisfied. The tabs across the top of the screen allow you to alter (in order, from left to right) Settings, Body Shape, Facial Features, Hairstyle, Eyebrows, Eyes, Nose, Mouth, and Extra facial features such as beards, moles, and glasses. Features of each Mii creation page are detailed in the next pages.

Choose a look-alike: Creates a screen full of randomly generated Mii characters. If one of them looks like the character you want to create, select that face. If not, go "Back" and then re-enter this screen to generate all new faces. After you choose a face, a second screen appears displaying faces that are similar to the one you chose. This allows you to fine-tune your Mii to better resemble the character in your imagination and to give yourself an even greater head start in the New Mii creation process.

MAKING MY MII

The rest of this section is described from a first person point of view, as I guide you through the steps I took to create the Mii you see depicted in the screenshots. When I was finished creating this Mii, I asked the opinions of other people around the Nintendo offices and they thought it bore a fair resemblance to me. And when I finished this one, I made another Mii that looks like my wife. If I can succeed, so can you!

8

MII CHANNEL

Tab 1: Mii Settings

When creating a new Mii, the first tab allows you to create a profile for the Mii. All settings on this page are optional. Several of these settings determine how your Mii interacts with other Miis:

Nickname: Give your Mii a distinctive name. My name is Dan, and so I named my look-alike Mii "Doodle." I thought it was funny at the time....

Favorite?: Point at this box and press Ⓐ to indicate whether this Mii is a Favorite. Favorites are grouped separately from other Mii characters, so choose your Favorites wisely. Wait to determine whether a Mii is a Favorite until you've finished working on its appearance. If the results are great, then return to this page and make your awesome Mii a Favorite.

Gender: This option allows you to change your mind about the character's sex during the creation process. Male characters wear shirts and pants, while female characters wear mini-dresses.

Birthday: Determine the Mii's birthday. First set the month, then the date. I input my own birthday since this Mii is actually supposed to be me. But you can choose a friend's birthday or a celebrity's birthday if that is who you are trying to create. Otherwise, if the Mii is a wholly original creation, you should probably choose today's date. That way, every year your Mii can celebrate the day it was created by you!

Favorite Color: Choose the Mii's favorite color, which also determines its shirt or dress color. Mii characters' bodies tend to change shape and appearance depending on what activities they engage in while being used in certain games. For instance, in *Wii Sports* Boxing, Mii characters wear boxing gear instead of the clothes you see on the New Mii creation screen. So don't get too hung up on picking a favorite color if you find it hard to decide.

Mingle: Point at this button and press Ⓐ to toggle mingling on or off. Mii characters set to mingle can copy themselves to other Wii consoles connected to the Internet and join in the Mii Parades on those consoles. If you don't want people to see your Mii, then choose "Don't Mingle."

Mii Creator: If you are proud of your work on your Mii, let others know! Point at this button and press Ⓐ to enter your name as the creator of this Mii.

Tab 2: Body Shape

The second page of options changes the body shape of your Mii creation. While pointing at the buttons of the sliders displayed on this page, press and hold Ⓐ to grab the button. Then aim the Wii Remote to the left or right to slide the button in the desired direction.

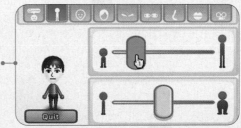

The top slider changes the Mii's height. Slide the button to the left to make the Mii shorter, or slide the button to the right to increase height. I'm not necessarily a short person, but I thought it would be funny to make my Mii short. I can't really explain my humor at times....

The bottom slider changes the Mii's body shape. Slide the button to the left to make the Mii skinny, or slide the button to the right to make your Mii nice and plump. I work out hard, so I thought it important that my Mii look fit as well.

QUICK REFERENCE

9

MII CHANNEL

TAB 3: FACIAL FEATURES

At the top of the facial features page are two buttons. The left button allows you to choose from eight basic face shapes. To make this Mii resemble my actual face, I chose a facial shape based on my jaw line.

The right button at the top of the facial features page allows you to add facial characteristics, such as makeup, freckles, dimples, five o'clock shadow, and old age wrinkles. And no, I don't have any wrinkles!

The six colored buttons on the screen's right side allow you to change your Mii's skin tone.

TAB 4: HAIRSTYLE

The fourth page of options contains 72 hairstyles to choose from. Because "curly fuzzball" wasn't one of the options, I chose a hairstyle that matches my messy appearance closely enough.

On the screen's right side are color options, varying from black to blonde or completely gray. The button below the color options allows you to move the part in the Mii's hair to the other side of its head.

[TIP]
ROTATING Mii
Once you've chosen a hairstyle, rotate your Mii to make sure that your hair looks good from every angle. To rotate the Mii, move the hand cursor over the Mii and press Ⓐ to make it spin around. This function helps to ensure that you haven't accidentally chosen a ponytail hairstyle if you don't have a ponytail!

CELEBRITY MiiS

ALI G

ARNOLD SCHWARZENEGGER

OPRAH WINFREY

MII CHANNEL

Mii Channel

Tab 5: Eyebrows

The fifth tab on the New Mii creation menu allows you to choose eyebrow shape and color. The buttons in the screen's bottom-right corner allow you to raise or lower the eyebrows, enlarge or decrease them in size, rotate them inward or outward, and separate or join them in one unibrow. My eyebrows aren't necessarily thick or pointy—maybe deep down, I wish they were—but I chose this eyebrow shape because my intention was to create a funny caricature of myself rather than something true to life.

Tab 6: Eyes

The sixth tab from the left contains eye shapes and sizes you can apply to your Mii. Four pages of eye shapes provide 48 options. The six options in the upper right corner change iris color. In real life, my eyes are actually hazel with a big brown blot in one corner of my left eye. But my bizarre pigmentation wasn't an option in the New Mii creation menu. So I chose to give this Mii green eyes, because it is the color most evident when I look at pictures of myself.

Tab 7: Nose

The seventh page of options allows you to change the shape and size of your Mii's nose. Several of the nose shapes are extremely abstract, which should make for some comical creations. The buttons on the right allow you to move the nose up or down on the face, and enlarge or decrease the nose's size. Originally I chose the first nose shape, because it's the closest to the form of my own. But then I figured it would make this Mii more comical looking to give him a completely non-distinct, upturned nose. I probably should have gone back to my original choice before saving this Mii....

Tab 8: Mouth

The eighth page of options allows you to choose your Mii's mouth shape and size. Certain mouths have full, colored lips. For these mouths, choose one of the three color options on the right to change the shade of gloss. The color cannot be changed on any mouth that is purely black. Use the buttons below the color choices to raise or lower the mouth's position on the face, or to enlarge or decrease the mouth size. I chose this mouth shape because I rarely give a big, toothy grin in photos. I'm something of a smart-alec, as my wife will confirm, and I feel like this mouth enhances the smarmy quality I wanted to capture in my Mii.

QUICK REFERENCE

11

MII CHANNEL

QUICK REFERENCE

TAB 9: EXTRAS

The last page of appearance options allows you to add facial hair, glasses, sunglasses, and a mole to your Mii. To add something like a goatee beard to your Mii, add both a mustache and a chin beard. For glasses there are six color options for the frames, and for beards there are eight color options. I used to wear a goatee myself; I wore one for 10 years, in fact. But recently I shaved it down to a chin beard because it's gone almost completely gray. Yes, I'm old. So I chose to color this Mii's beard gray to indicate something about my age.

QUIT

When your Mii masterpiece is finished, point the Wii Remote at the "Quit" button in the screen's bottom-left corner and press Ⓐ. On the subsequent menu, choose "Save & quit" to save the Mii to your console and send your Mii to the Mii Plaza, there to dwell with other Mii characters in peace and harmony forever and ever. Or, choose "Quit without saving" to scrub changes you might not be happy with, or to give up on your Mii altogether. Creation is tough, no matter what the medium, so don't feel bad about a few false starts!

Mii PLAZA

Once you have created a Mii, it is dropped into Mii Plaza, the large room where the Miis saved on your console congregate and mingle. Point the Wii Remote at the screen to cause menu options to appear along the sides of the screen. Point at the icons to display the function of each:

On the left side of the screen:

Wii Menu: Return to the main Wii Menu.

Edit Mii: Make changes to an existing Mii character. Point at a Mii and press Ⓐ + Ⓑ simultaneously to grab it. Then drag it over to the Edit Mii icon on the left side of the screen to enter the Mii creation menu.

New Mii: Create a new Mii from scratch or from a look-alike.

Erase Mii: Permanently delete a Mii. This cannot be undone, so make sure not to delete the wrong Mii by mistake! Point at a Mii and press Ⓐ + Ⓑ simulta-neously to grab it. Then drag it over to the Erase Mii icon on the left side of the screen to send it to oblivion.

Help: View the Mii Plaza controls.

12

Mii CHANNEL

And on the right side:

Mii Parade: View Mii characters that have been transferred from people's Wii consoles through the Internet.

Transfer Mii: Save a Mii to your Wii Remote controller. Up to 10 Miis can be saved on one controller. Then you can take your controller to a friend's house and use your Mii to play on their Wii console. To save a Mii to a Wii Remote, pick it up and drag it onto one of the empty circles on the controller. Dragging a Mii onto an occupied circle kicks out the old Mii.

Wii Friend: This option appears after friends are added to the Wii Message Board address book. You can send Miis to your friends using this button. Press this button to make an envelope appear onscreen. Drag a Mii onto the envelope, and then choose one of the addresses in your address book.

Arrange: Point at the whistle in the bottom right corner and press Ⓐ to command the Miis wandering around the screen to line up for your viewing pleasure. The slide-out menu tells you how many Miis are in Mii Plaza and allows you to arrange them in alphabetical order or in groups by Favorites, by color, or by gender.

Mii PARADE

While viewing the Mii Plaza screen, point at the Mii Parade icon in the screen's upper-right corner and press Ⓐ to go to the Mii Parade on your console. The Travel settings must be set to "Travel" for Miis from other people's consoles to congregate here. And for your amusement, they will march in a parade. If your Wii console unit is not connected to the Internet, then this screen serves no function. Point the Wii Remote at the screen to bring up menu icons:

On the left side of the screen:

Send to Mii Plaza: All Mii characters appearing in the Mii Parade screen are there only temporarily; the next time you turn on your system, they may have moved on to someone else's console! To save a Mii character to your console permanently, point at it and press Ⓐ + Ⓑ to grab it. Then drag it over to this icon on the screen's left side to save it to your console.

Erase Mii: If some of the Miis in the Mii Parade are irritating you, then pick them up and drag them over to this icon on the screen's left side to permanently remove them from the parade. This does not mean you will never see them again, however....

And on the right side of the screen:

Mii Plaza: Go back to the Mii Plaza screen.

Travel Settings: Determine whether or not to allow Mii characters from other consoles to congregate on your console, and whether to let your Miis travel to other consoles.

Speed: Toggle the movement speed of the parade, either walking speed or running speed. This also changes the speed of the marching drum.

CELEBRITY MiiS

QUICK REFERENCE

13

[PHOTO CHANNEL]

Photo Channel allows you to view and edit photos and videos stored on SD memory cards compatible with digital cameras and cell phones. Photo Channel also allows you to post photos to the Wii Message Board for others in your household to view.

After selecting Photo Channel from the Wii Menu, point at the "Start" button and press Ⓐ to initiate Photo Channel.

At this point, insert a SD memory card containing photos or motion jpeg format video (.MOV or .AVI files) into the SD card slot on the front face of the Wii console. Slide the SD memory card in until it clicks into place.

On the first screen, choose the first option to view and edit photos and videos stored on the SD memory card inserted into the console. Choose the second option to view and edit photos and videos posted on the Wii Message Board.

THUMBNAIL MENU

Whether you view photos on an SD memory card or on the Wii Message Board, the control scheme is the same. Press ⊖ or ⊕ to zoom out or in, respectively.

- Zooming out allows you to view more photo thumbnails onscreen at once. You can zoom out until every photo stored on the card is visible onscreen, albeit tiny in size.
- Zooming in allows you to see the photo or video composition more clearly, but reduces the number of photos that can be viewed at one time.
- You can zoom in on the Thumbnail Menu until only one picture is shown at a time, in large scale!

Point at any of the bottom options and press Ⓐ to select one:

Back: Return to the storage selection menu.
Arrows: Scroll down or up through thumbnails. Or hold Ⓑ and aim the Wii Remote at the center area to scroll up or down.
Slide show: View photos one at a time in a slide show, with various options available as detailed below.

PHOTO CHANNEL

SLIDE SHOW OPTIONS

While a slide show is in progress, point the Wii Remote at the screen and press Ⓐ to pause. From the options displayed, choose "Back" to quit the slide show or choose "Change settings" to change the appearance of photos or videos during the slide show:

Resume slide show: Point at this option and press Ⓐ to resume viewing photos in slideshow format.

Order: Point at the "Change" button at the right side of this line on the Slide-show Settings menu and press Ⓐ to cycle through two options: show the pictures in order by "Date" or show pictures at "Random."

Effects: Changes the manner in which pictures are displayed and moved onscreen: "Dramatic" zooms in on the picture or zooms out while the picture moves to one side or the other; "Simple" shows the pictures full screen, with gray bars at the sides or top if needed; "Nostalgic" moves the pictures the same as the Dramatic setting, but in grayscale with a sepia filter applied to create an aging effect.

Music: Set the mood by choosing a song to be played during the slide show. While perusing this menu, choose the "Other music" option in the bottom-right corner to play an MP3 song copied to the SD memory card inserted into the console. To copy an MP3 song to an SD memory card, you must have either a laptop or desktop PC with an SD card slot, a USB SD card reader, or a printer with an SD card slot in order to copy MP3 format music to the card.

 PHOTO/VIDEO VIEWER

To view a single photo or video, use the Wii Remote to point at it in the thumbnail viewer and press Ⓐ. The selected photo or video fills the screen. Point the Wii Remote at the screen to cause menu bars to appear at the top and bottom of the screen:

Zoom ⊖: Point at this button and press Ⓐ to zoom out and reduce the size of the photo or video onscreen. Or press ⊖ on the Wii Remote.

Rotate: Point at the button with two circling arrows and press Ⓐ to rotate the picture 90 degrees.

Next: Advance to the next photo stored on the SD memory card or Wii Message Board.

Zoom ⊕: Point at this button and press Ⓐ to zoom in and increase the size of the photo or video onscreen. You could also press ⊕ on the Wii Remote.

Back: Point at this button and press Ⓐ to return to the thumbnail viewer screen. You could also point the Wii Remote at the center of the picture and press Ⓐ.

Post: Post the displayed photo to the Wii Message Board for safekeeping and for other members of your household to view. Photos saved to the Wii Message Board can be attached to messages and sent to friends via the Internet.

Fun!: Point at this onscreen button and press Ⓐ to enter the Fun! menu, with the options: Mood, Doodle, and Puzzle.

Slide show: View photos one at a time in a slide show, with various options available as detailed above.

[TIP]
FUN! MENU EASTER EGG
While viewing the Fun! menu, point the cursor toward the lower part of the screen and hold it there. Soon, a small black cat should move across the yellow bar at the top of the screen. Quickly move the hand cursor onto the cat and press Ⓐ to grab it before it escapes. If you successfully catch the cat, which we lovingly refer to as "Miiow," it provides tips on using Photo Channel!

QUICK REFERENCE

15

QUICK REFERENCE

MOOD

The Mood menu allows you to apply effects to the entire photograph or video at once.

"Brighten" changes the luminosity of the photo, increasing the brightness in eight stages. To return to the original brightness, simply select the "Brightness" button enough times to return to normal.

"Black and White" converts the image or video to grayscale. Simply press the same button again to return to color, if possible.

[NOTE]
If you do a mood change on a video file, the sound of the video changes as well!

"Zap!" creates a negative image of the photo or video, reversing all colors as shown in the screenshot.

"Hard-boiled" converts the image to a grainy black and white cartoon, similar to the digital effects seen in the movie *Sin City*. The Hard-boiled effect can be increased by eight stages.

DOODLE

The Doodle Menu allows you to point at the screen with the Wii Remote and draw directly onto the photograph or video, using a variety of pencil types. The standard pencils are displayed across the top of the screen, with seven colors to choose from. But you are not limited to these colors; select the eye-dropper tool on the left side of the upper menu bar to select any color from within the photo as your paint color. To draw, select a pencil, the eye dropper, or the eraser, then point the Wii Remote at the screen and hold the Ⓐ button.

To increase the thickness of your drawing lines, move the Wii Remote closer to the television screen. To draw thinner lines, pull the Wii Remote back away from the display. Try using a variety of lines to make one of your friends look like Mario or another Nintendo character.

Along the bottom of the Doodle menu are four stamps that enable you to draw lips, sunglasses, stars, and hearts on the photo. To place big sunglasses or a big kiss on the subject in your photo, move the Wii Remote closer to the television screen. To place small hearts or small stars on the photo, move the Wii Remote farther away from the display.

To rotate the angle of the object to be drawn onscreen, turn the Wii Remote in your hand while keeping the top end pointed at the screen. This technique allows you to place hearts at various angles, or to place sunglasses on the bridge of someone's nose, as I have done to Prima Games author Steve Stratton in the screenshot.

PHOTO CHANNEL

Use the scissors tool to select a circular area of the photo to copy. Move the scissors cursor to one point of the photo, then press and hold Ⓐ while dragging a circle around the area to be copied. Release the Ⓐ button to draw the copied area onto another part of the photo, creating a mirror image effect or psychedelic look!

To erase all changes made to a photo, select "Undo all" in the screen's bottom right corner. A rocket ship flies across the screen and sweeps away all your changes!

[T I P]
PHOTO ANONYMITY
Point the Wii Remote at a photo displayed onscreen and press either ✛ or ✛ to create a pixelation effect on a photograph, similar to what many reality shows do to obscure individuals' faces.

PUZZLE

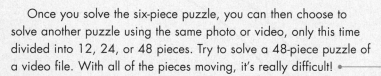

The Puzzle option of the Fun! menu converts any photo or video file into a six-piece puzzle for you to solve. Point the Wii Remote at the puzzle pieces and press Ⓐ to grab them. While holding a piece, move the Wii Remote across the screen to drag the puzzle piece into place. You can also use the arrows at the bottom of the screen to move the entire puzzle up, down, left, or right by one row. Point at and select the "Cheat" button in the screen's lower right if you need a reminder of what the photo originally looked like. The program times you to see how fast you can solve the puzzle, and also keeps track of how many times you cheat!

Once you solve the six-piece puzzle, you can then choose to solve another puzzle using the same photo or video, only this time divided into 12, 24, or 48 pieces. Try to solve a 48-piece puzzle of a video file. With all of the pieces moving, it's really difficult!

QUICK REFERENCE

17

PHOTO CHANNEL

[WII SHOP CHANNEL]

After connecting your Wii to the Internet and performing an update, you can access the Wii Shop Channel. This exciting channel allows you to purchase and download Virtual Console channels, Internet Channels, and other exciting downloads by redeeming Wii Points.

Point the cursor at the Wii Shop Channel on the Wii Menu and press Ⓐ to enter. Select the "Start" button to begin shopping online.

WELCOME SCREEN

After a brief connection period, the welcome screen appears. The welcome screen displays not only the "Start Shopping" button, but also a row of Virtual Console games. Either select the "Start Shopping" button to proceed to the main screen, or select one of the tiny thumbnails to learn more about a game that you might be interested in downloading.

MAIN MENU

The main menu screen of the Wii Shop Channel allows you to (from the top left):

- Shop for Virtual Console games
- Download new channels and "Wii Ware"
- "Add Wii Points" to your account
- Check "account activity"
- Change your "settings"
- Return to the "Wii menu"
- View a complete "shopping guide"

WII SHOP CHANNEL

VIRTUAL CONSOLE

Virtual Console allows your favorite games from the past to come back to life on the Wii. All games are rated "E" for "everyone." On the main screen, you may choose one of the following sorting methods:

- Display "games from one game system"
- List games alphabetically regardless of system or release date
- Show titles by "newest additions" first
- Show "titles you've downloaded" to review

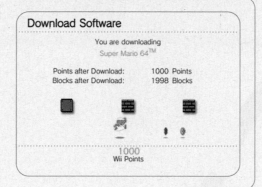

Download Software

You are downloading
Super Mario 64™

Points after Download: 1000 Points
Blocks after Download: 1998 Blocks

1000
Wii Points

Games are available from the following classic systems:

Nintendo Entertainment System (500 points each)
Super Nintendo Entertainment System (800 points each)
Nintendo 64 (1,000 points each)
SEGA Genesis (800 points each)
TurboGrafx (600 points each)

[TIP]
Notice that the download screen shows Mario running across the screen. As the download progresses, Mario jumps up and knocks coins loose from platforms over his head. Much better than a standard download progress bar, don't you think?

[NOTE]
Nintendo of America has pledged that new Virtual Console games shall become available for purchase and download every Monday. Therefore, check in every week and view the "newest additions" to see what is available!

19

Wii WARE

The Wii Ware menu features channels and other software available for the Wii, such as the Internet Channel Trial Version and other software that may become available. Most Wii Ware channels must be purchased using Wii Points, although free trial versions of software may also be available.

Wii Ware

Internet Channel Trial Version

Google

Google is a trademark of Google Inc.

Browse the Web with family and friends from the comfort of your living room! Use the Wii Remote to navigate the Internet with this trial version of the Internet Channel.

Because this is a trial version of the Internet Channel, certain functions that are available in the final version are restricted in this version. Nintendo's liability for any damage arising from using the Internet Channel is limited as set forth in the Wii Network Services Agreement.

Back   2000
          Wii Points   Download

To download Internet Channel Trial Version, select the Download button. More information regarding the Internet Channel is detailed later.

ADD Wii POINTS

Virtual Console games and Wii Ware can be downloaded in exchange for Wii Points. Buy Wii Points at a rate of 100 points/$1.00. Wii Points have no cash value and are redeemable only for Wii Virtual Console games and Wii Ware software.

How does one obtain Wii Points? By purchasing Wii Points Cards with cash at video game and electronics retailers, or by purchasing them using a credit card through a Wii connected to the Internet.

REDEEM WII POINTS CARD

To redeem a Wii Points Card purchased at a video game or electronics retailer, choose the "Redeem Wii Points Card" option. Look on the back of the Wii Points Card and notice a silver scratch-off area. Scratch away the silver to reveal the Points Card activation number.

Point the Wii Remote cursor at the white box below "Wii Points Card Activation Number" and press Ⓐ to enter the number. Type in the number exactly as you see it on the back of the card. The number of points purchased (usually 2,000 or $20 worth) will be added to your account.

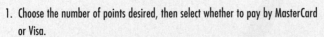

BUY WII POINTS WITH A CREDIT CARD

Choose this option on the Add Wii Points menu to purchase Wii Points with a credit card. If Parental Controls are active, a parent must enter the pin number password to enable this feature. Then follow the steps in order:

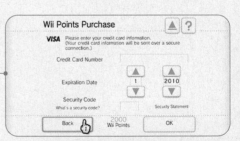

1. Choose the number of points desired, then select whether to pay by MasterCard or Visa.
2. On the following screen, enter the 16-digit credit card number by pointing at the top white box and pressing Ⓐ.
3. Use the arrows to change the expiration date to the date shown on the front of the credit card, month and year.
4. Point at the small white box next to "Security Code" and press Ⓐ. Enter the security code from the back of the credit card.
5. Select "OK" to continue. After a brief transaction approval, the points purchased are added to your account. Wii Points remaining are displayed on all menus of the Wii Shop Channel.

WII SHOP CHANNEL

[NOTE]
The security code is a special three-digit number printed inside the signature box on the back of the credit card. This is provided as an extra security measure to prevent fraudulent use of your credit card account. This code as well as your credit card account number are not retained by Nintendo of America and are used only to validate a one-time transaction.

ACCOUNT ACTIVITY

Enter this menu to review all transactions posted on your account. Press the button on any transaction in the "Content" column to view a receipt for the transaction or a description of the product downloaded.

SETTINGS

Options in the Settings menu allow you to link your Wii Shop Channel account to your My Nintendo account so you can track your Wii purchases through *www.nintendo.com*. Note that frequent shopping at *nintendo.com* sometimes entitles you to bonuses, bonus merchandise, and other benefits.

The other option in this menu allows you to delete your Wii Shop Channel account, voiding all Wii Points remaining and disavowing all rights to downloaded software. This might be an option to consider if you are selling your Wii to another person, because Wii Points are non-transferable. This option is also a great way to punish bad children!

QUICK REFERENCE

21

WII SHOP CHANNEL

[FORECAST CHANNEL]

After performing an Internet update, Forecast Channel becomes available. Forecast Channel enables you to view the current weather conditions in your area, as well as a five-day forecast as determined by the Weathernews Image satellite of NASA. You can also view the temperature in various parts of the world!

[CAUTION] To continue receiving forecast updates, please enable WiiConnect24 through the Wii Settings menu as described in the "Hardware Setup and Menus" section.

INITIAL SETTINGS

After downloading Forecast Channel, confirm the time and date. Then select your state and the nearest major city or population center from a list of areas. Weather information for the area selected is the default that appears each time Forecast Channel is started.

FORECAST SCREEN

After getting a few settings out of the way, Forecast Channel is yours to play with. The main screen displays the temperature and weather conditions in your area or in the closest city.

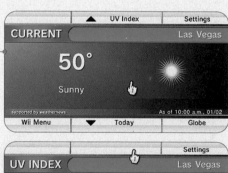

On the main screen, press ✛ to view the Ultraviolet (UV) Index for the day to determine if you should wear sunscreen outside. The UV Index indicates just how strong the rays of the sun should be in your area. If you live in Nevada, as the author of this book does, monitoring the daily UV Index is essential to avoiding skin cancer. The same may be true in your area as well.

Press ✛ to view today's forecast, detailing what the highest temperature and the most severe

weather should be all day long. The wind information in the screen's lower right indicates how strong winds shall be and wind direction.

22

FORECAST CHANNEL

Press 🔂 again to view tomorrow's prediction for weather. Press 🔂 one last time to see a five-day forecast for your area.

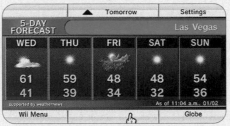

[T I P]
The Home menu features a complete Operations Guide for the Wii Forecast Channel. Please refer to it if you have further questions.

SETTINGS

Point the Wii Remote at the Settings button in the screen's upper right and press Ⓐ to make changes to Forecast Channel's display. The closest location, temperature display, and wind display can all be changed.

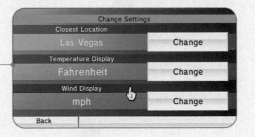

GLOBE

Point the Wii Remote at the Globe button in the screen's lower right and press Ⓐ to view the world as seen from NASA's Weathernews Image satellite. At first, the image is zoomed in to show your immediate area. Press ⊖ to zoom out. You can continue zooming out until the entire planet is displayed onscreen! Press ⊕ to zoom back in.

Point at any of the locations displayed onscreen to view weather for that area. The current weather situation for every location in the world is available. However, forecast information may not be available outside your area.

QUICK REFERENCE

FORECAST CHANNEL

23

Rotate the globe to view other regions of the planet. Point the Wii Remote cursor at any place outside of a location on the globe. Press and hold Ⓐ to grab the globe, and then move the Wii Remote to rotate the display.

Initially, current weather symbols are displayed next to each major location. Press ✚ to change the symbols to current temperature readings. Press ✚ repeatedly to cycle through today's weather prediction, today's high temperature, tomorrow's weather prediction, and tomorrow's high temperature before going back to the current weather.

Use the rotate buttons at the bottom of the globe display to rotate the world upward for a more topographical view of regions or the entire planet.

When finished viewing the globe, point the Wii Remote at the End button in the screen's lower-left corner and press Ⓐ to return to your local weather information. On the local weather screen, point the Wii Remote cursor at the Wii Menu button in the screen's lower left to return to the main menu.

[TIP]
As the Operations Manual indicates, you can grab the globe and spin it a strong flick of the wrist while holding a Wii Remote.

[N E W S   C H A N N E L]

As of the publication of this guidebook, News Channel is not yet available. The concept of News Channel is to provide a news feed gathered from the Associated Press and provide news bulletins to users regarding local and national news headlines.

FORECAST CHANNEL

NEWS CHANNEL

[INTERNET CHANNEL TRIAL VERSION]

Internet Channel allows users to surf the Internet using Google search. For a limited time, Wii owners may download a trial version of Opera Powered™ Internet Channel without spending Wii Points. The true version of Internet Channel should be available in 2007. The trial version has limited functionality that may or may not be part of the final product.

DOWNLOADING INTERNET CHANNEL

Open the Wii Shop Channel and select the Wii Ware button in the screen's upper right. Select the "Download" button to begin downloading the Internet Channel Trial Version. Internet Channel installs itself, then restarts the Wii system.

BROWSER CONTROLS

- Ⓐ Select highlighted option. Used to click on links or browser buttons.
- Ⓑ Hold and move Wii Remote to scroll page in any direction.
- ⊕ Zoom in. Enlarges page on the screen.
- ⊖ Zoom out. Reduces page size on the screen.
- ⌂ Home Menu. Change controller settings or return to the Wii Menu.
- ① Favorites Menu. Allows you to open frequently visited pages quickly.
- ② Switch display mode. Changes the page layout to single column mode with large letters, making some Web pages easier to read. Press again to return to normal layout.

START PAGE

Select Internet Channel on the Wii Menu. When Internet Channel takes over the screen, press the Start button in the screen's lower-right corner to initialize the program.

The first page that appears is the Start Page. This page presents three options: •

Favorites: Displays a page of favorite links and webpages. It's preprogrammed with pages such as *www.wii.com* and *www.opera.com,* home of Opera Browser, which serves as the basis for Internet Channel.

Enter a Web Address: Brings up the virtual keyboard, allowing you to enter a web address. Enter all addresses as *"www.somewebpage.com"*. There is no need to add *"http://"* before the address.

Help: Select this option to view the Wii Remote controller layout and button functions.

> **[TIP]**
> Scroll down on the Start Page if you wish to read the user's agreement. Hold Ⓑ and move the Wii Remote controller to scroll. Press ⊕ to zoom in on the fine print, and press ⊖ to zoom out to normal view.

THE BROWSER BAR

The bar running horizontally across the bottom of the screen contains several buttons that perform various functions:

1. **Back:** Return to the previous webpage.
2. **Forward:** Return to the next webpage. You must have used the Back button to make this button functional.
3. **Reload:** Refresh the currently displayed page. This is useful when browsing Internet message boards to see if new messages have been posted.
4. **Favorites:** Open the Favorites page.
5. **Start Page:** Return to the Internet Channel Start Page.

INTERNET CHANNEL
Enter a Web Address

ADDING A FAVORITE

To add a page to your Favorites screen:

1. Click on the "Enter a Web Address" button on the Start Page.

3. Wait for the page to load completely. Select the "Favorites" button in the browser bar at the bottom of the screen.

2. Type the desired web address using the virtual keyboard, in the format *"www.somewebpage.com"*.

4. Select the first button from the left, "Add Favorite," to add the current page to your Favorites screen.

QUICK REFERENCE

27

INTERNET CHANNEL

Enter a Web Address

[VIRTUAL CONSOLE CHANNEL]

Virtual Console games downloaded through the Wii Shop Channel become channels all their own on the main Wii Menu. Play any Virtual Console game by pointing at it with a Wii Remote controller and press Ⓐ. On the title screen, select the "Start" button to begin the game.

Many classic Virtual Console games require the Classic Controller to play. Please check the details page for a game to determine if the Classic Controller is required before downloading a Virtual Console game from the Wii Shop Channel. Plug the Classic Controller attachment into the base of the Wii Remote controller. Set the Wii Remote on a coffee table or the floor, and point it toward the television and sensor bar to transmit a wireless signal.

The awesome *Super Mario 64* is new again thanks to the Virtual Console.

[T I P]

Press the Home button (⊙) while playing Virtual Console games to pause the game anywhere, anytime. The Home screen features a re-creation of the original game instruction manual so that you may learn every facet of playing a Virtual Console game.

VIRTUAL CHANNEL

QUICK REFERENCE

28

Virtual Console Channels Available (as of 1/1/2007):

Nintendo Entertainment System
Baseball
Donkey Kong
Donkey Kong Jr.
Ice Hockey
Mario Bros.
Pinball
Soccer
Solomon's Key (TECMO)
Super Mario Bros.
Tennis
The Legend of Zelda
Urban Champion
Wario's Woods

Super Nintendo Entertainment System
F-Zero
Street Fighter II: The World Warrior (CAPCOM)
Super Castlevania IV (Konami)

Nintendo 64
Super Mario 64

Sega Genesis
Altered Beast
Columns
Dr. Robotnik's Mean Bean Machine
Ecco the Dolphin
Golden Axe
Gunstar Heroes

Sega Genesis continued
Ristar
SimCity
Sonic the Hedgehog
Space Harrier II
Toe Jam & Earl

TurboGrafx16
Alien Crush
Bomberman '93
Bonk's Adventure
Military Madness
R-TYPE
Super Star Soldier
Victory Run

QUICK REFERENCE

VIRTUAL CHANNEL

29

WII SPORTS

30

QUICK REFERENCE

31

Wii SPORTS

[BASEBALL BASICS]

Baseball is a game where one team takes to the field while the other is "at bat." Players at bat, known as "batters," attempt to strike a baseball and knock it into the outfield to gain enough time to run around the bases, or knock the baseball into the stands for a home run. The team at bat scores whenever a batter hits a home run or runs across home plate. The team in the field meanwhile attempts to catch the ball before it hits the ground, attempts to tag players while they are off-base, or the pitcher of the field team attempts to "strike out" the batters. A *Wii Sports* Baseball game is only three innings, unless one player scores five points more than the other, in which case the game mercifully ends.

Indeed, baseball is a complex game with complex rules. Fortunately in *Wii Sports* Baseball, all you have to worry about is pitching or batting; the game controls the rest of the field team automatically. This section of the guide explains everything you need to know to become a *Wii Sports* Baseball pro.

32

BASEBALL

STARTING BASEBALL

To begin a game of *Wii Sports* Baseball, insert the *Wii Sports* disc into the Wii console unit. On the Wii menu, point the Wii Remote hand cursor at the Disc Channel (now displaying "*Wii Sports*") and press Ⓐ.

Highlight the Baseball button on the *Wii Sports* startup menu. Press Ⓐ while pointing at the Baseball button to begin a three-inning game of baseball.

NUMBER OF PLAYERS

Choose whether to play with one or two players. To play baseball with a friend, wirelessly connect two Wii Remote controllers to the Wii console unit. Each player must have his or her own controller.

MII CHOICE AND HANDEDNESS

Next, pick out the Mii character you want to represent yourself on the field. Choose from any of the Miis stored on your system or on an SD memory card inserted into your Wii console.

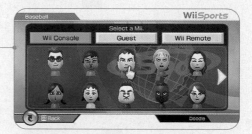

Choose which hand you will use to control the game: which hand you will bat with, which hand to pitch with, etc. These choices also change your Mii character's stances at the plate and on the pitcher's mound.

[Mii AT BAT!]

Use Mii Channel to create a Mii character before starting a baseball game. If a Mii character is not available on your Wii Remote or in the flash memory of the Wii console, the game prompts you to create one. The Mii Channel creation menu opens. For explanation of Mii character creation, refer to the "Welcome to Wii" section toward the front of this book.

BASEBALL

QUICK REFERENCE

33

BASEBALL

ONSCREEN DISPLAY

1. **Balls:** The number of throws ruled as balls because they did not cross the plate and the batter did not swing.
2. **Strikes:** The number of strikes against the current batter. Includes up to two foul balls.
3. **Outs:** The number of outs against the team currently at bat.
4. **Diamond:** Displays where base runners are standing in the field, if any.
5. **Mii Batter:** That's you!
6. **Inning:** The current inning.
7. **Team Captain:** An icon of your Mii's face is displayed here, and the face of the other team's captain is displayed on the opposite side.
8. **Score:** The current score. It goes up every time a batter crosses home plate.

CONTROLS

QUICK REFERENCE

Swing Wii Remote: swing bat/pitch ball

⬆, ⬇: Hold while pitching to throw over the plate

⬅, ➡: Hold while pitching to throw inside or outside the plate, depending on the batter's stance

Ⓐ: Pitch curveball

Ⓑ: Pitch screwball

Ⓐ+Ⓑ: Pitch splitter

BATTING STANCE

There are two possible stances for controlling the batter's swing: either stand parallel to the television and swing the Wii Remote like a bat, or sit down and raise the Wii Remote near your face to make your Mii raise his/her bat. Then swing the Wii Remote downward and point at the screen to swing.

Either stand and swing the Wii Remote as shown, or...

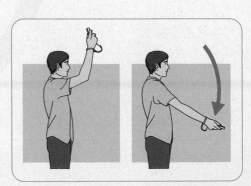

...sit and flick the Wii Remote at the screen as shown here.

HERE'S THE PITCH...

To pitch the ball, make one of two motions: either make an overhand throw gesture while holding the Wii Remote as you would to throw a baseball in real life, or raise the Wii Remote in front of your face, then point at the screen. The latter option allows you to play while seated.

Make an overhand throwing motion as you would when pitching a ball, while holding the Wii Remote tightly.

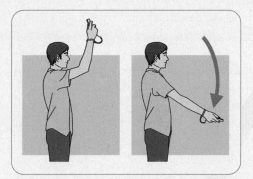

Pitch with the same motion as batting, and while seated.

PITCH TYPES

Change your pitch's angle by holding certain buttons while making a pitching motion. Put some spin on the ball by throwing a curveball or a screwball to increase the chances that the batter will miss or knock a foul ball.

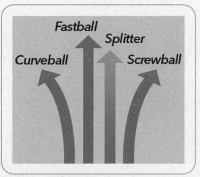

Ⓐ: Pitch curveball
None: Pitch fastball
Ⓐ+Ⓑ: Pitch splitter
Ⓑ: Pitch screwball

[TIP]
Pitch Underhand
To pitch in an underhand style, press ②. Press ① to return to normal pitching style.

35

BASEBALL

PLAY DETERMINATION

When the batter hits a fair ball, the fielders and outfielders do their best to catch or grab the ball as soon as possible.(Any ball that flies into the field or outfield inside the first base and third base lines is considered a "fair ball.") The play is determined by how long it takes the fielding team to gain control of the ball. If the ball is caught before touching the ground, the batter is out. If the ball rolls into a fielder's glove, the batter may be called out because the fielder could reasonably throw the ball to first base before the batter arrives there. If the ball goes into the outfield and is not caught out of the air, the batter may score single, double, or triple plays depending on how long the outfielders take to capture the ball.

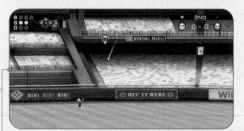

To increase the chances of getting a single, double, or triple play, the batter must attempt to knock the ball as far into the outfield as possible, into a zone with less coverage. This should reduce the chances of a pop fly being caught. If the outfielders have to chase the ball, at least a single play is scored. The batter and all base runners advance one base. But if the fielders drop the ball or take a long time to pick it up, there's a chance of scoring a double or triple play, where all base runners get to advance two or three bases, respectively.

[THE ULTIMATE PLAY!]
With two or more base runners in the field, hitting a home run is more important than ever. Knocking the ball into the stands or out of the park allows all base runners and the batter to score!

[NOTE]
The other Miis you've created and saved to your console make up the rest of your teams. Be sure to create Miis of people you've always wanted to play ball with.

36

BASEBALL

BASEBALL TRAINING

HITTING HOME RUNS

A pitcher throws you 10 balls one at a time. Every pitch is a fastball over the plate, enabling you the best shot at hitting a home run. The objective is to hit as many home runs as possible. The difference between the Platinum and Gold requirements

is that you must knock the ball out of the park several times, thus accumulating the total feet required.

HITTING HOME RUNS TRAINING MEDALS

Medal	Home Runs
Platinum	10 (5,175 ft. total)
Gold	10
Silver	8
Bronze	5

SWING CONTROL

Target zones are displayed on the field as you swing at 10 pitches. Strike the ball so you knock it into the dark blue zone to score the most points. The target zone starts off right up the middle. Then it moves to left field. To strike balls into left field, swing early to hit

the ball. For the last three balls, the target zone moves to right field. Knock balls into right field by swinging late to hit the ball.

SWING CONTROL TRAINING MEDALS

Medal	Score
Platinum	65
Gold	55
Silver	40
Bronze	25

BATTING PRACTICE

A pitcher throws 30 fastballs your way, and the goal is to hit as many fair balls as possible. Your batting arm will be sore after this!

BATTING PRACTICE TRAINING MEDALS

Medal	Hits
Platinum	30
Gold	27
Silver	20
Bronze	15

QUICK REFERENCE

37

BASEBALL

BASEBALL TERMINOLOGY AT-A-GLANCE

Ball: A pitch outside the strike zone, which the batter identifies and does not swing at. After four balls, the batter advances to first base, and any base runners take an additional base.

Base Runner: A player previously at bat, now standing on first, second, or third base after hitting the ball.

Batter: The player who stands at home plate and tries to hit the baseball with a baseball bat.

Curveball: A pitch that veers to the left when thrown with the right hand, or veers to the right when thrown with the left hand.

Fastball: A straight pitch thrown across the plate as fast as possible.

Fielder: All players standing within the baseline, including the catcher, pitcher, basemen, and shortstop.

Foul Ball: A ball batted outside the first base line or third base line. The first two foul balls count as strikes against the batter.

Inning: Both teams have a turn at bat and in the field. *Wii Sports* Baseball ends after three innings.

Inning Top: Also "top of the inning." The first half of an inning when player one gets to bat and player two must pitch.

Inning Bottom: Also "bottom of the inning." The second half of an inning, when player two gets to bat and player one must pitch.

Out: Each team gets three outs in an inning. Team players are out (in *Wii Sports* Baseball) under the following circumstances:
- The batter accumulates three strikes.
- The batter strikes the ball and it is caught by a fielder before it touches the ground.
- The batter fails to reach first base before a fielder acquires the ball and can reasonably toss it to the first baseman before the batter arrives.
- A base runner fails to advance to the next base before a fielder throws the ball to the second or third baseman, or to home plate.

Outfielder: Defensive players standing in the green area outside the field, hoping to catch a pop-fly ball.

Pitcher: The player in the field who throws the ball across home plate for the batter to strike.

Screwball: A pitch that curves to the same side as the hand from which it was thrown. For a right-handed pitcher, the ball curves to the right, and vice versa for a left-handed pitcher.

Splitter: A pitch thrown in such a manner as to make it act unpredictably, usually by applying spit or grease.

Strike: The batter fails to strike a ball pitched directly over home plate.

Walk: After four balls, the batter gets to walk to first base. A base runner standing on first base advances to second, and so forth.

BASEBALL

Wii Sports Bowling

[BOWLING BASICS]

IN BOWLING, THE OBJECTIVE IS TO ROLL A BOWLING BALL DOWN A LANE, ATTEMPTING TO KNOCK DOWN 10 PINS ARRANGED IN A TRIANGULAR FORMATION AT THE FAR END. THIS SECTION EXPLAINS HOW TO BOWL LIKE A PRO.

[ROLL WITH Mii!]
If you do not have a Mii character saved to your Wii Remote or saved on the flash memory of the Wii console, then the game takes you straight into the Mii Channel creation menu. For explanation of Mii character creation, please refer to the "Welcome to Wii" section.

QUICK REFERENCE

39

BOWLING

STARTING A BOWLING GAME

On the *Wii Sports* main menu, point the Wii Remote at the "Bowling" button onscreen and press Ⓐ to begin a game.

For bowling instruction and practice, point the Wii Remote at the "Training" button in the screen's lower-right corner and press Ⓐ. Three exercises are available. Use these exercises to develop the skills necessary to roll like a pro or to win training medals by setting high scores.

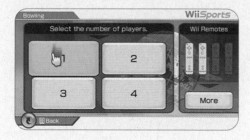

[CHANGE BALL COLOR]
Sick of the same old bowling ball every game? Change the color of the ball by holding the Control Pad in a certain direction as the screen fades from black just after pressing Ⓐ to clear the dangerous objects warning:

⬆: blue ball

⬇: green ball

➡: red ball

⬅: gold ball

QUICK REFERENCE

NUMBER OF PLAYERS

Select from one to four players to play a game. To connect more Wii Remotes, press Ⓐ on the player-one remote and temporarily connect more players by selecting the "Reconnect" button. Then press ① + ② simultaneously on each remote to add. Each player can connect his or her own Wii Remote, or multiple players can share one remote.

BOWLING

CONTROLS

Swing Wii Remote: Roll bowling ball.

Ⓑ: Hold to approach lane and release during swing to roll ball.

Ⓐ: Toggle aiming mode between angle/position.

⬆: Zoom in on pins at end of lane.

⬅: Rotate angle left/step left.

➡: Rotate angle right/step right.

ONSCREEN DISPLAY

1. **Actions:** Shows button commands available at any time.
2. **Pin Map:** Displays the pin formation. Use this to determine if one pin is hiding behind another.
3. **Mii Character:** That's you!
4. **Aim Guidelines:** Shows if you can sidestep left or right, and also shows angle of throw.
5. **Lane Line:** Throw the ball before the Mii character arrives at this line or you must start over.
6. **Scorecard:** Displays score per rounds in standard bowling scoring format.

[TIP]
CURVING THE BALL

Curve in your roll tends to result from either purposely or subconsciously holding the Wii Remote at an angle during your throwing motion. Either straighten your rolls by consciously pointing the Wii Remote straight at the television set while throwing, both when pulling your arm back and while bringing it forward; or sidestep to the side before rolling to compensate for the curve in your roll so that the ball spins back to the middle, landing in the sweet spot between the 1 and 3 pins. In fact, learning to curve the ball into that sweet spot (the 1 and 3 pins if throwing right, the 1 and 2 pins if throwing left) is a great way to boost your strike count.

AIMING AT THE PINS

Before throwing the ball, determine whether to adjust your stance and aim. If the ball tends to curve when you throw, move a step or two to the left or right so that the rolling ball curves back to the center. This should increase your chances of a strike.

You can also change the angle of throw. Simply press Ⓐ to switch the aiming mode from sidestepping to angling. Angling your throw is a little trickier, and it's usually only necessary in training exercises when ob-stacles block the lane. It may also prove useful when aiming for a single pin standing on the edge of the lane when going for a spare!

QUICK REFERENCE

41

THROWING THE BALL

When you are positioned correctly and ready to throw, raise the Wii Remote level with the bottom of your chin. Press and hold Ⓑ on the bottom of the controller. The Mii character onscreen starts advancing toward the lane line. As the Mii moves, gently swing the controller back, and then swing forward toward your television set. As you pass the bottom of your swing, release Ⓑ to release the ball.

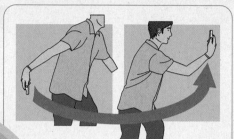

[TIP]
A rather amusing Easter egg in bowling occurs if you release Ⓑ while your arm is pulled back with the bowling ball. The ball drops behind the player, and the camera changes angles to show everyone screaming in horror!

[CAUTION]
If the ball rolls too slowly down the lane, you may be releasing Ⓑ too soon. If the ball flies through the air and lands on the lane with a hard thud, you are releasing Ⓑ too late. Either of these mistakes can add unwanted spin to your throw, which may cause the ball to curve.

SCORECARD

The scorecard is displayed in the screen's upper-right corner. The top number in the blue box is the round. A game consists of 10 rounds.

The number below that to the left is the score on the first ball. If the first ball rolls a strike, then an "x" mark appears in the box. The score is 10 points, plus the total number of pins knocked down in the next two rolls. Therefore, rolling three strikes in a row causes the first frame to be worth 30 points.

The score for the second ball is to the right of the first ball score. If the player picks up a spare on the second ball, half the box becomes filled. The score is 10 points, plus the total number of pins knocked down in the next roll. For instance, if a player rolls a spare, no score is entered in the box. If the player knocks down seven pins in the next roll, then the total score for the frame where a spare occurred will be 17. Thus, a spare can be worth up to 20 points.

The bottom portion of the box is the accumulative score, or the score thus far. The player with the highest cumulative score wins!

A perfect score of 300 consists of rolling 12 strikes in a row. The two extra strikes come from being able to roll up to three times in the final frame.

[TIP]
Score enough points (1,000) to reach pro level, and you will unlock a special bowling ball with a checkered design!

[B O W L I N G   T R A I N I N G]

Train yourself in playing *Wii Sports* Bowling, or challenge yourself to score a medal in these extra challenges. Choose "Training" from the main menu. There are three bowling training exercises.

PICKING UP SPARES

The objective of this training exercise is to score a spare by knocking down a few standing pins. Each lane has one more pin than the last, all the way up to nine. The player has five balls to play with. If you score a spare, then you get to keep your ball for the next lane. If you miss or fail to knock down all the pins, you lose a ball. Once you clear all nine lanes, the training starts over with a one-pin lane as long as balls remain.

PICKING UP SPARES TRAINING MEDALS

Medal	Lanes Cleared
Platinum	20
Gold	17
Silver	12
Bronze	7

POWER THROWS

The objective is to knock down as many pins as possible in 10 throws. After each throw, the lane becomes wider and more pins are added. The number of throws remaining and the number of pins knocked down are displayed in the screen's upper-left corner. Score all strikes to reach the top score and receive a Platinum Medal!

POWER THROWS TRAINING MEDALS

Medal	Pins
Platinum	700
Gold	600
Silver	500
Bronze	450

QUICK REFERENCE

43

BOWLING

SPIN CONTROL

This exercise challenges your ability to bowl around obstacles set in the lanes. Adjust your aim guideline using sidestepping and angling until you have a clear shot at the pin(s). Curve your throws to go around obstacles by twisting the Wii Remote slightly as you swing your arm to throw.

Here's an easy one: simply sidestep to the left or right, depending on how the ball curves when you throw.

Toss a curving ball to go around the obstacle and take down the pin!

Here's a much harder lane several rounds later. First sidestep and angle the aiming guideline so that the ball will pass through the two obstacles.

Then let her go with a slight spin on the ball. It goes through the obstacles and curves right at the pin!

SPIN CONTROL TRAINING MEDALS

Medal	Lanes Cleared
Platinum	20
Gold	17
Silver	12
Bronze	7

[NOTE]
There really is a trick-shot bowling tournament that determines if players can knock down pins behind obstacles! Look for it on ESPN and other sports networks!

BOWLING

BASIC BOWLING TERMINOLOGY AT-A-GLANCE

Gutter: The small depression on either side of the lane, designed to keep the ball from rolling back into the lane.

Gutterball: When the bowling ball rolls into the gutter without hitting any pins.

Pin: Standing white objects arranged in a triangle formation at the far end of the lane. The objective is to knock down all the pins in one or two rolls.

Spare: Knock down all of the pins by rolling two balls. A slash mark is recorded in the upper-right corner square of the score sheet for that frame. No score is entered until the first ball of the next frame is determined. At that point, the score on the first ball is added to the original 10 and entered as the score for the previous frame where the spare occurred, unless a strike occurs. Examples are elaborated later in this section.

Strike: Knock down all pins with the first ball. An "x" mark is recorded in the upper-left corner square of the score sheet for that frame. No score is entered until the player rolls the two balls of the next frame. Thus, the eventual score is 10 plus the total pins knocked down in the subsequent frame. Examples are elaborated later in this section.

[BOXING BASICS]

IN BOXING THE OBJECTIVE IS TO PUMMEL YOUR OPPONENT WITH PUNCHES UNTIL HE OR SHE IS KNOCKED UNCONSCIOUS AND CANNOT GET BACK UP. ANOTHER WAY TO WIN IN BOXING IS TO STAY CONSCIOUS FOR THREE FULL ROUNDS AND SCORE HIGHER WITH THE JUDGES THAN YOUR OPPONENT. THIS SECTION EXPLAINS EVERYTHING YOU NEED TO KNOW ABOUT HOW BOXING WORKS IN *WII SPORTS*, AND HOW TO ACHIEVE PRO STATUS IN NO TIME!

[PUNCH Mii OUT!]

If a Mii character is not saved to your Wii Remote or saved on the flash memory or on an SD card inserted into the Wii console, then the game takes you straight into the Mii Channel creation menu so that you may create an avatar. For an explanation of Mii character creation, please refer to the "Welcome to Wii" section near the front of this book.

QUICK REFERENCE

STARTING A FIGHT

On the main menu, point the Wii Remote at the "Boxing" button onscreen and press Ⓐ to begin a game.

For practice at becoming a better boxer, point the Wii Remote at the "Training" button in the screen's lower-right corner and press Ⓐ. Three boxing training exercises are available. Use these training programs to develop the ability to "float like a butterfly, sting like a bee." Win training medals by setting high scores.

45

BOXING

TAKING ALL COMERS

Next up, select the number of players. One player can play alone against a CPU-controlled fighter, or two players can play against each other. Each player must have his or her own Wii Remote with Nunchuk attachment.

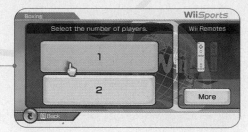

The next step is to select a Mii as your boxer. If no Mii characters are stored on your Wii Console's flash memory or on an SD memory card inserted into the unit, then you may choose to either enter the Mii Channel creation menu or choose a randomly generated Mii from the Guest page. Another option is to select a Mii stored on your Wii Remote.

Finally, choose whether to play boxing right-handed or left-handed. Be sure to hold the Wii Remote in your dominant hand and hold the Nunchuk in your other hand.

CONTROL

Control of a boxer in a boxing match is completely movement-oriented. Aside from pressing Ⓐ+Ⓑ or Ⓐ when prompted to advance through menus, there are no button combos to press. The sections below describe boxing with the motion-sensitive controllers.

BLOCKING

At all times, stand facing the television screen and the sensor bar and hold both controls up in front of your chin as depicted below. This is a blocking stance, which allows your character to block most punches and jabs. Raise the controls a little higher to block a punch aimed at your face. Lower the controller in front of your ribcage to block a jab aimed at your sides. From this position, strike out with punches and jabs.

PUNCHING

Punches are blows aimed at the opponent's head. To throw a right hook, move your right hand toward the screen while holding a controller. To throw your left, move your left hand toward the screen with a controller.

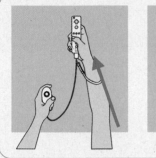 

Hold the controllers as shown if you are right-handed, and thrust one controller forward to perform a punching action.

Here is the punching action from a side view.

[TIP]
COMBOS: To perform a combo, start pumping the controllers in and out from your chest, moving one forward and back, and then the other. By pumping the controllers rapidly, you tell the console that you wish to perform a combo. Combos are extremely devastating in a boxing match. However, being able to perform combos is entirely dependent on your physical fitness level. Consult your doctor if the boxing program causes heart palpitations or shortness of breath.

QUICK REFERENCE

JABS

Perform jabs by holding the controller down at your side, then moving the controller forward at a low height. This causes your boxer to aim a jab at the opponent's ribcage. This is a great way to get around an opponent's defenses. If the opponent is holding his hands high, get him to lower his guard by performing jabs. When his head is unguarded, return to performing punches and try to knock him out!

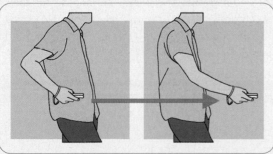 

Perform a jab by moving a controller from your side outward toward the television and sensor bar, at a low height.

47

BOXING

DODGING PUNCHES

Dodge punches by leaning left, right, or backward while holding both controllers in close to your body. The sensor bar reads your position and makes the onscreen character lean in the same direction. Use leaning to dodge punches from your opponent.

[TIP]

LEANING STRATEGY: Sometimes a CPU-controlled opponent leans to the right or left and stays there. This opponent is employing a lean strategy to make him or herself harder to hit while still being able to land punches with the uppermost hand. To counter this strategy, lean in the same direction, or mirror the lean. Then use your uppermost hand to punch and use your lower hand to jab.

ROUNDS

A boxing match lasts three rounds if both players remain conscious. Each round is three minutes long. The bell rings to signal the beginning and end of each round.

Players are scored during each round for their ability to land punches on the opponent. Knocking down an opponent for a short time scores major points.

If the boxing match lasts for all three rounds, then the winner is determined based on the number of punches landed and the number of times each player was knocked down.

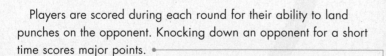

BOXING

48

PLAYER HEALTH

Each boxer's health is displayed as a circular pie graph that appears near the player's head when he or she takes damage. Pieces of the pie graph flicker and disappear as consciousness slips away from a fighter.

While punching combos are easier to land than jabs, jabs tend to strike harder and reduce the opponent's health more quickly. Don't forget to incorporate plenty of jabs in your boxing style!

[BOXING TRAINING]

Enter the Training menu and select one of the three exercises in the Boxing category to develop your boxing skills and win training medals.

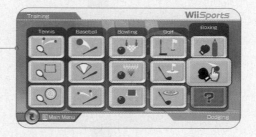

QUICK REFERENCE ▼

WORKING THE BAG

Destroy as many punching bags as possible within the time limit. The physical integrity of each punching bag is represented by a pie-shaped health graph, similar to a boxer's health graph. However, the bags are weaker than most of the opponents you face. The key is to pump the Wii Remote and Nunchuk back and forth in your two hands as rapidly as possible without abating. Once you build up combo speed, the bags should fall like dominoes!

WORKING THE BAG TRAINING MEDALS

Medal	Bags Destroyed
Platinum	40
Gold	35
Silver	26
Bronze	15

49

BOXING

QUICK REFERENCE

DODGING

Coach throws tennis balls at your head, and you must dodge them by leaning left or right to get out of the ball's path. You earn a point each time you dodge a ball. However, you lose a point each time a ball smacks you in the forehead!

DODGING TRAINING MEDALS

Medal	Points
Platinum	85
Gold	80
Silver	65
Bronze	50

THROWING PUNCHES

Your training coach holds up two mitts for you to hit. Aim your punches by pointing the Wii Remote or Nunchuk directly at the mitt your coach holds up. You earn a point each time you hit the mitt. However, you lose a point each time the coach takes a punch!

THROWING PUNCHES TRAINING MEDALS

Medal	Points
Platinum	70
Gold	60
Silver	45
Bronze	30

BOXING

Wii Sports Golf

[GOLF BASICS]

THE OBJECTIVE OF GOLF IS TO USE A GOLF CLUB TO KNOCK A GOLF BALL TOWARD THE HOLE IN THE GREEN AT THE FAR END OF THE FAIRWAY. THE PLAYER WHO CAN SINK THE BALL INTO THE HOLE USING THE FEWEST STROKES WINS.

WHETHER YOU ARE PLAYING NINE HOLES ON THE FAIRWAY OR ENJOYING TRAINING EXERCISES, THIS SECTION TELLS YOU EVERYTHING YOU NEED TO KNOW ABOUT PLAYING AND MASTERING WII SPORTS GOLF.

[USE YOUR Mii!]
Use Mii Channel to create a Mii character before starting a game of golf. If you do not have a Mii character saved to your Wii Remote or saved on the flash memory of the Wii console, then the game should prompt you to create one. The game then takes you straight into the Mii Channel creation menu. For explanation of Mii character creation, please refer to the "Welcome to Wii" section closer to the front of this book.

QUICK REFERENCE

51

GOLF

QUICK REFERENCE

STARTING GOLF

On the *Wii Sports* main menu, point the Wii Remote at the "Golf" button onscreen and press Ⓐ to begin a game of golf.

For golf instruction and practice, point the Wii Remote at the "Training" button in the screen's lower right and press Ⓐ. Three exercises are available. Use these exercises to develop the skills necessary to play golf or to win training medals by setting high scores.

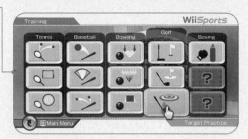

[TIP]
DISABLE ON-SCREEN DISPLAYS: Want to try golf without all the help? While on the "Select A Course" screen, hold ② as you make a selection. The mini-map and wind gauge disappear from the screen!

NUMBER OF PLAYERS

Select from one to four players to play a game. To connect more Wii Remote controllers, press ⊕ on the player-one remote and connect more remotes via the Home menu screen. Each player can connect his or her own Wii Remote, or multiple players can share a remote.

THREE HOLES OR NINE?

After selecting the number of players, choose whether to play a short game of three holes or to play nine holes. Choose depending on the amount of time you have to play.

GOLF

ONSCREEN DISPLAY

CONTROLS

Swing Wii Remote: swing club
Ⓐ: Strike ball
➕, ➕: Next club
➕: Rotate aim left
➕: Rotate aim right
①: View lay of the green, useful in putting
②: Change camera angle

1. Club: Depicts the club held. Club type affects driving range. Press ➕ or ➕ to change club.
2. Power gauge: Indicates power of swing. A straight blue interior indicates a controlled swing whereas a red squiggly interior indicates too much power in swing. Balls along the gauge indicate the distance your swing will drive the ball.
3. Mii character: That's you!
4. Stats: Displays hole, par, and yards or feet away from the hole.
5. Wind gauge: Shows the direction and speed of any wind that may influence flying golf balls. (Not displayed when putting.)
6. Course map: A mini overhead depiction of the golf course. Changes size and zoom depending on the type of club held. Flag marker indicates the hole position.
7. Distance gauge: Shows the aim of your drive, as in "where the ball should go when hit." Small balls along the gauge indicate distance. Change clubs to increase/decrease distance.

HOLDING THE WII REMOTE

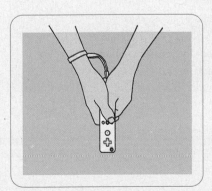

Hold the Wii Remote with both hands, as you would a golf club. Insert your wrist through the wrist strap to prevent accidentally dropping or throwing the controller. Hold the Wii Remote pointed down, with the left side of the controller facing the television set (if you are right-handed).

QUICK REFERENCE

53

GOLF

STANCE

Stand 3–15 feet away from the television screen, sideways, facing perpendicular to the display. Mimic the stance of the Mii onscreen. In this stance, you should be holding the Wii Remote down at your side with the left side of the controller facing the television screen (if you are right-handed).

AIMING YOUR SHOT

Press or to change the aim of your swing. As you press in either direction, the distance gauge on the course map changes angles to indicate where the ball should drive. If you swing too hard or angle your hand while swinging, the ball may slice or hook. Therefore, practice making a perfect swing to reduce curve in your drives.

Use the d-pad on the Wii Remote to change your driving angle, as indicated on the course map in the lower-right corner.

[TIP]
If your swing has a natural slice or hook that you cannot seem to overcome through practice, then change the aim of your shot to compensate for your innate style. If the ball is always hooking to the left, then change the angle of your drive to a few feet to the right of the hole.

If your arc always slices to the right, then move the distance gauge to the left to compensate for the natural curve in your shot. Pro golfers do it all the time!

DRIVING DISTANCE

Small ball markers along the distance gauge of the course map indicate how hard you must swing to drive the ball to that point on the map. For instance, if the distance gauge on the course map indicates that the ball is two measures away from the hole, then you must swing the club hard enough to raise the power gauge by up to two measures. If you swing too lightly, the ball falls short. Swing too hard and the ball may overshoot or go out of bounds.

Each time you prepare a shot, check the distance gauge to see how many markers lie between you and the hole. Practice swinging so that the power gauge fills to that point and no farther. Then mosey up to the ball and swing the Wii Remote the exact same way you did in practice.

GOLF

WIND COMPENSATION

If wind is a factor on the course, an arrow appears in the wind gauge in the screen's upper-right corner to indicate the wind's direction and speed. To reach the hole under such conditions, compensate for the wind by driving the ball *into* the gust. For instance, if the wind is coming in from the right, rotate the distance gauge to the right so as to hit into the wind.

Wind from behind can be beneficial. A gust from behind is sure to carry the ball farther and you need not swing so hard. Conversely, a draft from the front may slow the ball and reduce arc, shortening the drive.

CHANGING CLUBS

Press ✛ or ✛ on the Wii Remote to change clubs before a shot. Each club changes the distance gauge on the course map, indicating how short or far the driver, iron, or putter can reasonably knock the ball. Typically the game places the recommended golf club in your hands. However, there may be times when you want greater distance on a shot than what the recommended club allows.

PRACTICE YOUR SWING

The Mii golfer starts in the practice position next to the ball. Swinging the Wii Remote at this point causes the character to swing at the air. The power of the swing is displayed in the power gauge on the left side of the screen. Use the power gauge to determine how hard to swing to drive the ball as close to the hole as possible. Compare the power of your swing to the distance gauge on the course map in the screen's lower-right corner, and swing only as hard as needed.

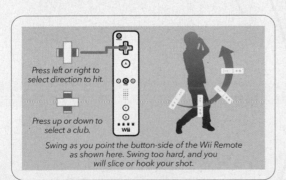

Press left or right to select direction to hit.

Press up or down to select a club.

Swing as you point the button-side of the Wii Remote as shown here. Swing too hard, and you will slice or hook your shot.

QUICK REFERENCE

55

GOLF

GOLF

While practicing your stroke, also check the wind gauge for possible interference, and change your angle of aim to compensate if needed. •

HITTING THE BALL

Swing the Wii Remote while holding down **Ⓐ**

Swing as you point the button-side of the Wii Remote as shown here.

When you're ready to hit the ball, press and hold Ⓐ to make the character step up to the ball. All gauges and maps disappear from the screen. Swing the Wii Remote while continuing to hold Ⓐ to strike the golf ball. Try to swing the Wii Remote exactly as you did during practice to ensure that the ball does not hook, slice, or fall short of the intended landing zone.

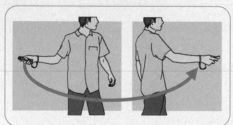

To drive the ball down the fairway or tee off, hold Ⓐ and raise the Wii Remote behind you. Then swing the controller downward and forward to strike the ball.

Swing through the ball to knock it down the fairway.

The viewing angle changes to follow the ball as it soars across the turf.

As the ball bounces to a stop, the power gauge remains onscreen to show you why the ball landed where it did. The landing area (fairway, rough, bunker, green) and the yards or feet left to the hole are displayed.

PUTTING

Once the ball lands on the green, the goal becomes to strike the ball just hard enough to knock it into the hole. The club to use is the putter, which should already be in your character's hand whenever you're on the green. The course map zooms in on the area surrounding the hole to help you gauge your shot. Practice your swing repeatedly before putting to make sure you hit the ball just lightly enough. Wind is not a factor in putting.

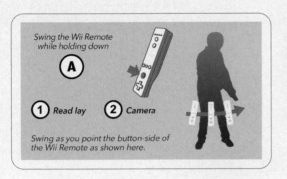

Another important factor to consider when putting is the lay of the green. Press ① to display the peaks and valleys on the green that might not be apparent to the naked eye. Light spots indicate a slope and dark spots show the dips. Slopes can affect the curve of the ball and pull it away from the hole. Compensate for dips and slopes on the green by changing your aim.

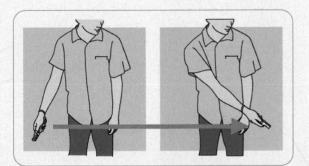

When putting, pull the Wii Remote backward only slightly, and then gently swing it forward without any speed. This should knock the ball lightly enough to go into the hole.

[TIP]

When attempting to putt the ball a very short distance, such as less than one measure on the distance gauge, try a "flick swing." Instead of pulling back the Wii Remote, hold it down at your side and lightly flick it forward. This prevents knocking the ball past the hole.

QUICK REFERENCE

57

GOLF

You and Wii™

[G O L F   T R A I N I N G]

To train yourself to play *Wii Sports* Golf, or to take on some extra golfing challenges, choose "Training" from the main menu. Three Golf training exercises are available.

PUTTING

The objective is to sink the ball into the hole with one putt. You get a point each time you score. Each player has five balls, displayed in the screen's upper-left corner. Each time you miss a putt, you lose a ball and must try again. There are 10 putting greens, so the highest score possible is 10 points without missing a shot.

QUICK REFERENCE

PUTTING TRAINING MEDALS

Medal	Points
Platinum	10 (No miss)
Gold	10
Silver	7
Bronze	5

GOLF

58

HITTING THE GREEN

This training exercise's objective requires you to chip the ball onto the green from a short distance away. Initially your ball may be located on the fairway, in the rough, or in a bunker just outside the green.

Hit 10 balls onto 10 different greens. Missing the green entirely means you must try again. The distance between the ball's resting spot and the hole determines scoring. The closer it lands to the hole, the better your score and the more likely that you will win a medal!

Because wind is not a factor in this exercise, scoring well is just a matter of aiming at the hole and swinging lightly enough to place the ball within range.

Perform a few practice swings before each attempt. Gauge your swing power by comparing the power gauge to the distance meter on the course map.

When measuring the power of your swing against the actual distance to the hole, it is better to swing a little short of the hole than right-on or too far. For example, if the distance to the hole is only three balls away as depicted on the course map, then swing only hard enough to drive the ball two and a half balls on the power gauge.

If you cannot seem to swing lightly enough to avoid slicing or hooking, try swinging the Wii Remote from behind to a downward-pointing position only. In other words, stop short on your swing to cause the ball to "pop" onto the green and roll close to the hole.

HITTING THE GREEN
TRAINING MEDALS

Medal	Feet to Go
Platinum	65.6 ft. or less
Gold	164 ft. or less
Silver	246 ft. or less
Bronze	492 ft. or less

QUICK REFERENCE

GOLF

QUICK REFERENCE

TARGET PRACTICE

This exercise focuses on making the ball bounce at a specific spot. Knock 10 balls so that they land on the target areas. The game marks the position where the ball first lands, and points are accumulated according to where the ball strikes on the target.

Target practice takes place on a hole with two floating greens. Although the farther green awards 100 points if you can bounce your ball in the target's center, hitting the outside rings of this target awards fewer points than a bounce anywhere on the closer target. Therefore, aiming for the closer target may create higher scores for beginners.

TARGET PRACTICE TRAINING MEDALS

Medal	Points
Platinum	800
Gold	600
Silver	400
Bronze	200

BASIC GOLF TERMINOLOGY AT-A-GLANCE

Birdie: A score of one stroke under par on a hole.

Bogey: A score of one stroke over par on a hole.

Bunker: A depression filled with sand, often called a sand trap.

Chip: A shot to the green from a short distance, accomplished with a low-impact swing to create a short arc.

Fairway: The green between the tee and the hole.

Green: The putting area around the hole.

Hook: The ball curves to the left for a right-handed golfer. The ball curves to the right for a left-handed golfer.

Par: The number of strokes set as a standard for a specific hole or a complete course.

Rough: The long grass surrounding the fairway.

Slice: The ball curves to the right if the golfer is right-handed. The ball curves to the left if the golfer is left-handed.

Tee: The starting or tee-off area of each hole from which the initial shot is hit. Also refers to the small wooden peg the ball is set upon when teeing-off.

GOLF

[TENNIS BASICS]

IN THE CASE OF *WII SPORTS* TENNIS, THE GAME IS A DOUBLES MATCH WHERE TWO TEAMS RALLY A TENNIS BALL BACK AND FORTH ACROSS THE CENTER NET ATTEMPTING TO SCORE POINTS. THE FIRST TEAM TO FAIL TO KNOCK THE BALL BACK ACROSS THE NET AND INSIDE THE COURT DEMARCATION LINES LOSES THE POINT TO THE OTHER TEAM. PLAY CONTINUES UNTIL ONE TEAM OUTSCORES THE OTHER.

TENNIS IS EASY TO PLAY, BUT IT HAS A COMPLEX SCORING SYSTEM. THIS SECTION FULLY EXPLAINS IT, ALONG WITH ALL THE INFORMATION YOU NEED TO HELP IMPROVE YOUR SWING AND MAKE YOU A TENNIS PRO!

QUICK REFERENCE

61

TENNIS

[SERVE Mii UP!]
Use the Mii Channel to create a Mii character before starting a game of tennis. If a Mii character is not saved to your Wii Remote, the flash memory of the Wii console, or an SD memory card inserted into the Wii, then the game should prompt you to create one. The game then takes you straight into the Mii Channel creation menu. For explanation of Mii character creation, please refer to the "Welcome to Wii" section at the beginning of this book.

QUICK REFERENCE

BEGINNING A MATCH

On the *Wii Sports* main menu, point the Wii Remote at the "Tennis" button onscreen and press Ⓐ to begin a game of tennis. •

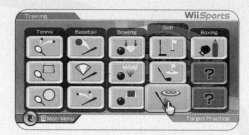

For tennis lessons, point the Wii Remote at the "Training" button in the screen's lower right and press Ⓐ.

Three exercises are available. Use these exercises to develop the skills necessary to play tennis or to win training medals by setting high scores in challenges.

NUMBER OF PLAYERS

One to four players can play in a tennis match, each person controlling one Mii character. Every player needs a Wii Remote of their own; players cannot share a controller. To synch controllers for additional players, click the "More" button beneath the Wii Remotes on the screen's right side. Press ①+② simultaneously on the next Wii Remote to synch with the console. Repeat for additional controllers. •

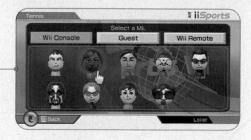

After choosing the number of players, select a Mii character to represent each person. You may use Miis stored on the system memory, on your Wii Remote control, or on an SD memory card inserted into the console. •

TENNIS

[TIP]
CHANGE THE COURT
Need a change of scenery? Hold ② after selecting Mii characters to change to the blue practice court from training. Now you don't have to feel the pressure of Wimbledon all the time!

CHOOSING POSITIONS

After you set up the game for all players, the next screen prompts you to select positions to control. When playing a single player or two-player game, your Mii should appear as the two Miis on one side of the court. If you do not wish for your Mii to be both players on the team, then highlight one of them and press Ⓐ to switch that position to a randomly determined Mii. In a three- or four-player game, Miis are assigned to certain positions and nothing can be changed. All that remains is to choose how many matches to play in your set.

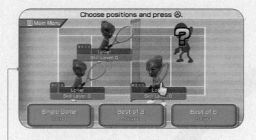

BEST OF THREE OR FIVE?

The final decision to make regarding your upcoming match is whether to play a single game, best of three, or best of five.

In a best of three game, the winner is the player or team who wins two matches. If a team loses the first two matches in a row, then the third match is not played.

In a best of five game, the winner is the player or team who wins three matches. If a team loses the first three matches in a row, then the fourth and fifth matches are cancelled.

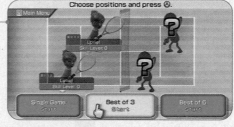

IMPROVE YOUR SWING (SANS TENNIS ELBOW)

To serve the ball with perfection, raise the Wii Remote in front of you to heft the ball into the air. While the ball is descending, swing the Wii Remote downward to serve the ball. Swing hard to make sure you clear the net!

[TIP]
THE POWER SERVE
If you get the timing just right, you can pull off a power serve. Toss the ball in the air and when it hits the peak of the lob (when it just hangs at the top of the throw), swing with a quick wrist flick. Get it all right and the ball will fire over the net at high speed. Ace! Your opponent will have to be on their toes to return a power serve.

QUICK REFERENCE

63

TENNIS

QUICK REFERENCE

When the ball approaches your Mii's position after the serve, prepare to swing your racquet to stroke the ball back over the net. If you are playing right-handed and the ball is approaching your Mii's right side, then perform a forehand swing using the Wii Remote to stroke the ball. If the ball is moving to the left side of your Mii, then prepare to perform a backhand stroke. If you are playing left-handed, then you'll perform a forehand stroke if the ball comes to your left and a backhand stroke if the ball bounces on your right.

During a forehand stroke, place your opposite shoulder toward the television screen and pull the Wii Remote behind you. When the ball bounces within range, swing the Wii Remote forward in an arc around your body, as shown below.

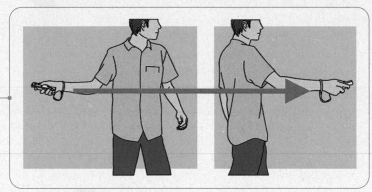

Forehand

During a backhand swing, place the shoulder of the arm you hold the Wii Remote with toward the television screen. Draw the Wii Remote back across your waist, and swing forward in an arc around your mid section.

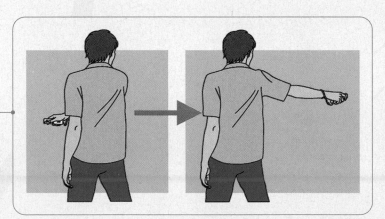

Backhand

64

TENNIS

When the racquet strikes the ball, the ball volleys away at an angle dependent upon the timing of your swing. Hit the ball too soon, and the ball may veer to the left if you are right-handed; hit the ball too late, and the ball may veer to the right.

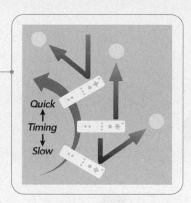

QUICK REFERENCE

TENNIS SCORING

If the opposing team fails to score, then your score should rise something like this:

15-0 (a.k.a., 15-*love*)
30-0 (30-love)
40-0 (Match point)
You win!

Should the opposing team manage to keep up with you score-wise, the score might work out something like this:

15-0 (15-love)
15-15 (a.k.a., 15-*all*)
30-15
30-30 (30-all)
40-30
40-40 (deuce)
40-Adv. (40-*advantage*)
You win!

In the example above, the teams were evenly matched until your team scored twice in a row, breaking the deuce and then taking the advantage point. However, if the opposite team had taken the advantage point, then the score would have gone back to deuce and resumed from there. Thus, the game of tennis is never truly lost until it's over, so don't give up!

TENNIS

TENNIS

[TENNIS TRAINING]

To engage in training exercises geared to improve your tennis playing, enter the *Wii Sports* training menu and select the "Returning Balls" training exercise. More tennis training exercises become unlocked as you complete the ones already open.

QUICK REFERENCE

RETURNING BALLS

The objective is to return balls across the net, into the opposing player's side of the court. The other player or the CPU character serves one ball after another. One point is scored for each ball returned into the court on the opposite side of the net. The first ball knocked out of bounds or not returned ends the training. Learning tennis couldn't be easier!

RETURNING BALLS MEDALS

Medal	Points
Platinum	80
Gold	50
Silver	25
Bronze	12

TIMING YOUR SWING

The objective is the same as for the Returning Balls training exercise, except that your returned ball must bounce through a moving goal on the other side of the court. If the ball fails to bounce inside the boundaries of the moving orange goal, then training ends. One point is scored for each ball returned through the moving goal.

TIMING YOUR SWING MEDALS

Medal	Points
Platinum	50
Gold	30
Silver	15
Bronze	7

TENNIS

TARGET PRACTICE

This exercise is all about controlling the direction of the ball. Return the ball repeatedly, striking the target each time. If you fail to hit the target, try to put some angle on the ball so that it flies back to the bull's-eye. Your Mii character runs to

position you properly to hit the ball each time, so all you must do is hit the ball with the right timing. Hit the ball a little soon to drive it to the left, and hit the ball a little late to make it sail right. One point is scored each time the ball strikes the target. Missing a stroke or knocking the ball on the other side of the court beyond the wall ends the exercise.

TARGET PRACTICE MEDALS

Medal	Points
Platinum	40
Gold	20
Silver	10
Bronze	5

[TIP]
GENERAL BONUS!
In *Wii Sports* Tennis and Boxing, achieving pro status (1,000 experience points) causes more Mii characters to appear in the stands during your games. Mii characters stored on your flash memory, Wii Remote, or an SD memory card inserted into the console are among the crowd!

BASIC TENNIS TERMINOLOGY AT-A-GLANCE

Advantage: The game point following deuce. If a team wins the advantage point, that team wins the game.

All: The score is tied below 40. For instance, a score of 15-15 would be called "15-all."

Backhand: For a right-handed player, hitting the ball on the left side of the body, and vice-versa for a left-handed player.

Ball Toss: The action of tossing a ball into the air when initiating a serve.

Deuce: Both teams have 40 points. The next team to score gets the advantage point.

Forehand: For a right-handed player, hitting the ball on the right side of the body, and for a left-handed player, stroking the ball on the left.

Love: A score of zero after a point is scored by one team; in other words, 30-0 would be pronounced "30-love."

Match Point: One team has scored 40 and is prepared to win the game because the other team has a lower score.

Mid-court: The area between the net and the service line, which the server is not to cross. Usually where the net player stands.

Net Player: The server's partner, who takes a position between mid-court and the net.

Net Rush: To aggressively move forward to a position near the net, or to "rush the net."

Out: The ball is served or returned and flies outside the side lines of the court before bouncing once. A score for the receiving team who allows the ball to go "out."

Rally: The ball is hit back and forth across the net between two or more players.

Serve: Every point begins with a serve. The server hits the ball over the net from a position behind the baseline. The ball must be hit diagonally across the court into the opponent's service court. The server gets two attempts to serve the ball correctly. The server alternates sides with every point.

Server: The player who serves the ball at the start of each point, then retains a position in the back court between the baseline and the service line in doubles.

QUICK REFERENCE

67

TENNIS

You and Wii™

QUICK REFERENCE

COMPANY HISTORY AND HARDWARE SETUP

68

HISTORY OF
NINTENDO

HARDWARE
SETUP

Wii

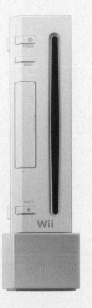

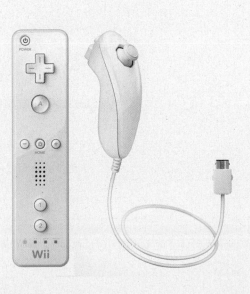

QUICK REFERENCE ▼

69

HISTORY OF NINTENDO

HARDWARE SETUP

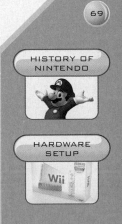

A Brief Corporate History of Nintendo

[COMPANY HISTORY]

QUICK REFERENCE ▼

NINTENDO CO., LTD., OF KYOTO, JAPAN, IS THE ACKNOWLEDGED WORLDWIDE LEADER IN THE CREATION OF INTERACTIVE ENTERTAINMENT. TO DATE, NINTENDO HAS SOLD MORE THAN ONE BILLION VIDEO GAMES WORLDWIDE, CREATED SUCH INDUSTRY ICONS AS MARIO AND DONKEY KONG AND LAUNCHED FRANCHISES LIKE *THE LEGEND OF ZELDA* AND *POKÉMON*. NINTENDO MANUFACTURES AND MARKETS HARDWARE AND SOFTWARE FOR ITS POPULAR HOME VIDEO GAME SYSTEMS, INCLUDING NINTENDO GAMECUBE AND THE GAME BOY SERIES—THE WORLD'S BEST-SELLING VIDEO GAME SYSTEM.

AS A WHOLLY OWNED SUBSIDIARY, NINTENDO OF AMERICA INC., BASED IN REDMOND, WASHINGTON, SERVES AS HEADQUARTERS FOR NINTENDO'S OPERATIONS IN THE WESTERN HEMISPHERE, WHERE MORE THAN 40 PERCENT OF AMERICAN HOUSEHOLDS OWN A NINTENDO GAME SYSTEM.

70

HISTORY OF NINTENDO

COMPANY TIMELINE

1889   Fusajiro Yamauchi began manufacturing "Hanafuda," Japanese playing cards in Kyoto.

1902   Mr. Yamauchi started manufacturing the first playing cards in Japan. Originally for export, the product became popular in Japan as well as abroad.

1933   Established an unlimited partnership, Yamauchi Nintendo & Co.

1947   Began a distribution company, Marufuku Co. Ltd.

1950   Hiroshi Yamauchi, grandson of the original president, took office as President and absorbed the manufacturing operation of Yamauchi Nintendo & Co.

1951   Changed the company name from Marufuku Co. Ltd. to Nintendo Playing Card Co. Ltd.

1952   Consolidated factories were dispersed in Kyoto.

1953   Became the first to succeed in manufacturing mass-produced plastic playing cards in Japan.

1959   Started selling cards printed with Walt Disney characters, opening a new market in children's playing cards. The card department boomed!

1962   In January, listed stock on the second section of the Osaka Stock Exchange and on the Kyoto Stock Exchange.

1963   Changed company name to Nintendo Co. Ltd. and started manufacturing games in addition to playing cards.

1969   Expanded and reinforced the game department; built a production plant in Uji City, a suburb of Kyoto.

1970   Stock listing was changed to the first section of the Osaka Stock Exchange. Reconstruction and enlargement of corporate headquarters was completed. Started selling the Beam Gun series, employing opto-electronics. Introduced electronic technology into the toy industry for the first time in Japan.

1973   Developed laser clay shooting system to succeed bowling as a major pastime.

1974   Developed image projection system employing 16mm film projector for amusement arcades. Began exporting them to America and Europe.

1975   In cooperation with Mitsubishi Electric, developed video game system using electronic video recording (EVR) player. Introduced the microprocessor into the video game system the next year.

1977   Developed home-use video games in cooperation with Mitsubishi Electric.

1978   Created and started selling coin-operated video games using microcomputers.

1979   Started an operations division for coin-operated games.

QUICK REFERENCE

71

HISTORY OF NINTENDO

QUICK REFERENCE

1980   Announced a wholly owned subsidiary, Nintendo of America Inc. in New York. Started selling "GAME & WATCH" product line.

1981   Developed and began distribution of the coin-operated video game *Donkey Kong*. This video game quickly became the hottest selling individual coin-operated machine in the business.

1982   Merged New York subsidiary into Nintendo of America Inc., a wholly owned subsidiary headquartered in Seattle, Washington, U.S.A., with a capital of $600,000.

1983   Built a new plant in Uji city to increase production capacity and to allow for business expansion. Established Nintendo Entertainment Centres Ltd. in Vancouver, B.C., Canada, to operate a family entertainment center. Raised authorized capital of Nintendo of America Inc. to $10 million. In July, listed stock on the first section of the Tokyo Stock Exchange. Started selling the home video game console "Family Computer" employing a CPU (Custom Processing Unit) and PPU (Picture Processing Unit).

1984   Developed and started selling the unique two-screen interactive coin-operated video game "VS. System."

1985   Started to sell the U.S. version of Family Computer "Nintendo Entertainment System" (NES) in America. The system included R.O.B.—Robotic Operating Buddy—and the games *Duck Hunt* and *Super Mario Bros.* Mario and Luigi became as big a hit as the NES.

1986   Developed the "Family Computer Disk Drive System" to expand the functions of the Family Computer. Began installation of the "Disk Writer" to rewrite game software. Game Counselors were organized and players from all over the world could call Nintendo for advice on games and strategies.

1987   Sponsored a Family Computer "Golf Tournament" as a communications test using the public telephone network and Disk Faxes to aid in building a Family Computer network. The NES achieved the status as the #1 selling toy in America and *The Legend of Zelda* became the first new-generation home video game to exceed sales of one million units.

1988   Nintendo of America Inc. published the first issue of *Nintendo Power* magazine in July. Researched and developed the Hands Free controller, making the NES accessible to many more Nintendo fans. The game library for the NES grew to 65 titles, helping to broaden the demographics to include more adults.

1989   Released *The Adventure of Link*, sequel to the top-selling game *The Legend of Zelda* in the U.S. Started "World of Nintendo" displays in U.S. to help market Nintendo products. Studies show that children are as familiar with Mario as they are with Mickey Mouse and Bugs Bunny! Introduced Game Boy, the first portable, hand-held game system with interchangeable game paks. *Nintendo Power* magazine became the largest paid-subscription publication in its age category.

1990   Nintendo Power Fest, featuring the Nintendo World Championships, tours the country. Japan enters the 16-bit market by releasing the Super Famicom in the fall.

HISTORY OF NINTENDO

1991 The 16-bit Super Nintendo Entertainment System (Super NES), along with *Super Mario World,* is released in the U.S.

1992 The Super NES *Super Scope* and *Mario Paint* with the Super NES Mouse Accessory were released. The long-awaited *Zelda* sequel, *The Legend of Zelda: A Link to the Past,* arrived for the Super NES. Nintendo of America Inc. developed portable Fun Centers to assist the Starlight Foundation in bringing happiness to hospitalized children by allowing them to enjoy their favorite video games during hospital stays.

1993 Nintendo announces the advent of the Super FX Chip, breakthrough technology for home video systems. The first game using the Super FX Chip, *Star Fox,* is released in April.

1994 The Super Game Boy accessory was released, expanding the library of games that could now be played on the Super NES! Everyone's favorite heroine, Samus, returns in another long-awaited sequel, *Super Metroid.* Nintendo helped pioneer the development and implementation of an industry-wide rating system. This year also saw the introduction of a game that would set a new standard in video game excellence. Using proprietary Advanced Computer Modeling (ACM) graphics, *Donkey Kong Country* took the holiday season by storm! Nintendo Gateway projected to reach 40 million travelers.

1995 Thanks to the outstanding success of *Donkey Kong Country,* ACM graphics were introduced to the Game Boy system by way of *Donkey Kong Land.* Along with this great boost to the Game Boy system line, Nintendo also introduced the Play It Loud! series of Game Boy systems. ACM graphics made another appearance on the Super NES with the release of the arcade smash-hit, *Killer Instinct.* At the same time, Nintendo introduced a 32-bit Virtual Immersion system known as the Virtual Boy. Next, Nintendo responded to the demands of fans with the release of *Yoshi's Island: Super Mario World 2.* Nintendo even enhanced the quality of ACM graphics for the upcoming release of *Donkey Kong Country 2: Diddy's Kong Quest. Cruis'n USA* and *Killer Instinct* were available in local arcades. Celebrated the one-billionth game pak being sold.

1996 Nintendo 64 launches in Japan on June 23. Thousands line up to be the first to experience the world's first true 64-bit home video game system. In early September, Nintendo introduces the Game Boy pocket, a sleeker, 30-percent smaller version of the world's most popular hand-held video game system. On September 29, Nintendo 64 launches in North America. *Super Mario 64* is proclaimed by many as "the greatest video game of all time!" For the Super NES we saw the release of the third game in the continuing Donkey Kong series, *Donkey Kong Country 3: Dixie Kong's Double Trouble.*

1998 Nintendo introduces Game Boy Color and innovative devices Game Boy Camera and Printer, bringing new life to the longest running hit in the history of interactive entertainment. *Pokémon,* a breakthrough game concept for Game Boy, was introduced to the world and generated a nationwide craze to collect 'em all! The most anticipated video game ever, *The Legend of Zelda: Ocarina of Time* for Nintendo 64 was released, setting new standards and breaking records for pre-sell for any video game to date.

QUICK REFERENCE

73

HISTORY OF NINTENDO

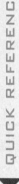
1999 The success of the Pokémon franchise expands even further with the release of *Pokémon Pinball*, *Pokémon Yellow*, and the first Pokémon title for the Nintendo 64, *Pokémon Snap*. Nintendo releases several notable N64 titles, including *Star Wars Episode 1: Racer*, *Mario Golf*, *Super Smash Bros.*, *Donkey Kong 64*, *Mario Party*, and *Perfect Dark*. At E3, Nintendo announces development plans for a new system, code-named Dolphin, that will utilize an IBM Gekko processor and Matsushita's proprietary optical disk technology.

2000 Nintendo sells its one hundred millionth Game Boy unit, ending the year with more than 110 million sold. Game Boy is responsible for 47 percent of all U.S. hardware system sales (an all-time high for a portable device). *Pokémon Stadium* is the top-selling console game, followed by *The Legend of Zelda: Majora's Mask*, both for N64. *Pokémon Gold* and *Silver* for Game Boy Color make their U.S. debut in October, becoming the fastest-selling games of all time by selling a combined 1.4 million copies in one week and 6 million through December.

2001

Beloved Nintendo characters Mario and Donkey Kong celebrate their 20th anniversaries. Nintendo launches its highly anticipated Game Boy Advance in Japan on March 21. The portable powerhouse debuts in the U.S. on June 11, and sells one million units in six weeks. Following the success of the Game Boy Advance, Nintendo launches the Nintendo GameCube home video game console in Japan on September 14. The U.S. launch on November 18 smashes previous U.S. sales records, becoming the fastest-selling next generation hardware system.

2002 After 52 years at the helm of Nintendo Co., Ltd., Hiroshi Yamauchi steps down and names Satoru Iwata his successor. Nintendo releases a slew of hot titles for the Nintendo GameCube including *Super Mario Sunshine*, *Mario Party 4*, *Animal Crossing*, *Eternal Darkness*, and the game that many laud as the greatest title of 2002, *Metroid Prime*. Nintendo releases their first online game for the Nintendo GameCube, *Phantasy Star Online*. By the end of 2002, more than 25 million Game Boy Advance units are in homes around the world.

2003 Nintendo takes an already successful system and makes it better, with the introduction of the Game Boy Advance SP. Its stylish flip-top design and rechargeable battery help it become the must-have system across all age groups. Following up the previous year's critically-acclaimed success of Nintendo GameCube titles, Nintendo launches *The Legend of Zelda: The Wind Waker*. The game's cell-shaded style breaks the mold and is hailed as one of the best Zelda games ever. Giving fans further ways to enjoy their Nintendo products, the release of the Nintendo GameCube Game Boy Player allows gamers to play their Game Boy and Game Boy Advance games on their televisions.

HISTORY OF NINTENDO

2004 Nintendo launches the innovative, new, dual screen handled video game system: the Nintendo DS. The Nintendo DS offers touch screen controls, wireless multiplayer, and backwards compatibility with Game Boy Advance games. The demand for the Nintendo DS makes it one of the year's hottest items. *Pokémon FireRed* and *LeafGreen* launch for the Game Boy Advance, continuing the success of the Pokémon franchise. *Metroid Prime 2: Echoes* hits the scene for the Nintendo GameCube, and is lauded by critics and fans alike.

2005 November saw a truly special moment in Nintendo's history: the launching of the Nintendo Wi-Fi Connection. Nintendo DS owners were treated to this free and easy-to-use wireless service that enabled them to play with other gamers from around the world. The service was so successful that after only two months from launching, over 10 million connections were made by nearly half-a-million unique users! On the GameCube front, the much-anticipated *Resident Evil 4* launched first on the Nintendo GameCube, earning "Game of the Year" honors from many publications, and setting a new standard in graphics and game play. After nearly 20 years of providing top-notch game play support, Nintendo transitioned its game play help resources from Game Play Counselors, to exclusively offering help on web sites, through publications, and on our pre-recorded Power Line. An improved Game Boy Advance SP, the sleek new Game Boy micro, and the innovative Nintendo DS kept Nintendo on top of the handheld market.

2006 November 19, 2006—Nintendo released the Wii home video game console in North America. And *you* are there!

QUICK REFERENCE

75

HISTORY OF
NINTENDO

QUICK REFERENCE

[NINTENDO CORPORATE CULTURE]

Nintendo of America is located in Redmond, Washington. Much of the translation and localization of many of America's favorite games occurs here. The marketing staff is also located here. Whenever you see a giant cardboard cutout of Mario, Link, or Pokémon at your favorite game store, those items were created at the offices in Redmond.

Inside the main office, employees enjoy lunch in the awesome Mario Café, where they can purchase food cooked to order. On certain days of the week, the cafeteria may also serve tacos, Chinese noodle soup, or Italian food prepared the way you like it. Plus there is a Starbucks® inside Mario Café, as well as a huge dessert bar! Providing a pleasant lunchroom environment for its employees encourages them to eat in the offices and be more productive.

CORPORATE
CULTURE

The pride, heritage, and history of the Nintendo of America company is on display in the Nintendo Museum on the second floor of the offices, right above the main entrance. The entire history of the company is etched into hanging glass panels, and one of each console released by the company is on display inside glass cases. The walls are lined with the various trophies Nintendo of America has won over the last several decades from retailers, youth groups, and charity organizations, to name a few. Box art of every game ever released on a Nintendo console is displayed on row upon row of shelves, and working kiosks allow employees to play various Game Boy, Game Boy Advance, and GameCube games on their breaks. There's even a lounge area with a wide-screen TV, a GameCube, and four wireless Wavebird controllers for anyone wanting to challenge a colleague to a friendly multiplayer game.

77

CORPORATE
CULTURE

Behind the Nintendo Museum is the Nintendo Fun & Games store, where employees and visitors can purchase Nintendo games, systems, clothing, accessories, and various other Nintendo and Nintendo character trinkets at a fraction of the retail price. Nintendo must be a fantastic place to work!

78

CORPORATE CULTURE

Hardware Setup and Menus

[WHILE YOU ARE AT THE STORE]

When purchasing the Wii from your favorite electronics retailer, be sure to ask a sales clerk to point you toward the Wii accessories. Purchasing a few additional components may be worthwhile:

- The composite AV cable included in the Wii console unit package is perfect for standard tube televisions with a 4:3 aspect ratio. But if you intend to play on a High-Definition (HD) widescreen television, then buy the **Wii Component Cable** sold separately.

- The Wii can connect to the Internet via a broadband wireless connection. To set up a wireless network in your home, visit a retailer that sells computers and networking equipment. A knowledgeable sales associate at the store can help you purchase the necessary equipment.

-  The Wii can also connect to the Internet via the **Nintendo USB modem** connected to a USB router or hub. The Wii USB modem allows the console to connect to the Internet via a wired connection.

- A **Nintendo Wi-Fi USB Connector** can also connect the Wii to the Internet. This is the easiest and cheapest connection option for those who own a PC with a wired connection to the Internet.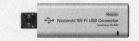

-  To download and play timeless Nintendo favorites such as *Mario Bros.* or *The Legend of Zelda,* we strongly recommend that you buy the **Wii Classic controller**. This controller has a more standard button layout and should increase playability and enjoyment of older titles purchased and downloaded through the Wii Shop Channel.

  The Wii Classic controller features a more standard button layout to increase comfort when playing older games. The Classic controller plugs into the bottom of the Wii Remote.

QUICK REFERENCE

79

AT THE STORE

[H A R D W A R E   S E T U P]

The first step to enjoying the Wii is proper setup. The next few sections aim to guide you in setting up your Wii console unit in your living space.

Your Wii console package should contain the following parts:

- Wii system
- Wii Remote controller with wrist strap
- Nunchuk controller attachment
- Sensor bar with connection cord
- Clear plastic sensor bar base
- Sheet of adhesives for sensor bar base
- 12V AC power adapter
- Composite cable
- Vertical console stand
- Console stand base
- *Wii Sports* game disc
- Instruction manuals, warranties, and limited-time offers from Nintendo

MR. TIDY HERE

When setting up consoles or any complex equipment, I find it useful to unpack all items from the box and lay them on a flat surface in a clear area for easier part identification while reading instructions and determining the first steps to take. This helps me to identify and locate parts quickly, with less frustration.

HARDWARE SETUP

CONSOLE PLACEMENT

Place the Wii console unit within seven feet of the television (so the composite cable can reach). When placing the Wii horizontally, make sure that the disc-loading slot is on the top of the faceplate.

The unit can lie flat on a sturdy surface, or it can stand on its right side using the included vertical stand. When placing the Wii in the vertical stand, place the Wii so that the GameCube controller ports and memory card ports are on the top of the console.

[CAUTION]
Situate the Wii in a well-ventilated area. Do not block the cooling fan vent on the back of the Wii, or the system may overheat. Do not submerse the Wii in water or place it where it might fall into aquariums or water fountains.

VERTICAL STAND ASSEMBLY

The vertical stand included in the box is a two-piece construction. Attach the clear plastic circular stand base to the gray console holder by inserting the prongs on the clear plastic piece into the holes on the bottom side of the stand. Then lock the stand base into place by sliding it backward until you hear an audible "click."

Place the angled back corner of the Wii console into the similarly shaped niche near the back of the vertical stand.

81

HARDWARE
SETUP

Wii

You and Wii™

QUICK REFERENCE ▼

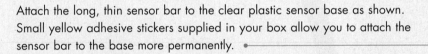

CONNECTING THE POWER CABLE

Plug the 12V power cable into a wall socket, or preferably into a connected surge protector. Insert the connector at the other end of the cable into the slot marked "12V=IN" on the back of the Wii console unit. One corner of the connector end is slanted, so align the connector to the slot appropriately.

[TIP]
A surge protector helps to prolong the life of all electronics in your house—especially televisions, DVD players, and video game consoles—by filtering electronic power so that power surges are less likely to damage equipment.

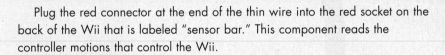

SENSOR BAR CONNECTION AND PLACEMENT

Attach the long, thin sensor bar to the clear plastic sensor base as shown. Small yellow adhesive stickers supplied in your box allow you to attach the sensor bar to the base more permanently.

Plug the red connector at the end of the thin wire into the red socket on the back of the Wii that is labeled "sensor bar." This component reads the controller motions that control the Wii.

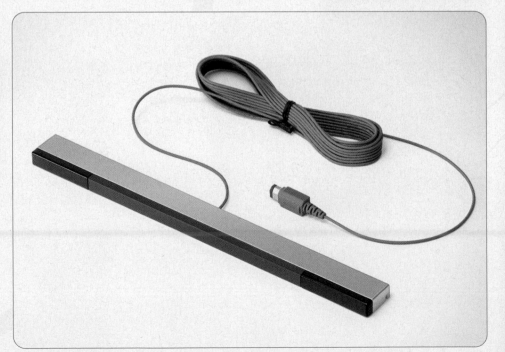

HARDWARE SETUP

Wii™

82

Place the sensor bar on top of your television, or directly below it, to enable better interaction with the screen. Make sure the sensor side of the sensor bar is facing the position where you and your fellow players will be seated or standing.

[CAUTION]
If the sensor bar is placed below your television and does not appear to be accurately reading motions made with the Wii Remote, it may be that the sensor bar is too low. Try placing the sensor bar above or on top of the television. Be sure to enter the Wii Settings menu and change the sensor bar placement from "Below TV" to "Above TV." Then return to your game and see if that improves the control.

[TIP]
As closely as possible, try to center the sensor bar in relation to the television display. This improves interactivity with onscreen action.

[TIP]
If placing the sensor bar below a television, place the sensor bar at the edge of the shelf the television rests upon.

QUICK REFERENCE

CONNECTING AUDIO-VISUAL CABLES

The Audio-Visual (or AV) cables connect the Wii to your TV. Included with the Wii is a composite AV cable.

Plug the AV jacks into the appropriate jacks on your television (usually found on the back of the TV). The video jack should be yellow while the audio jacks should be red and white. First, make sure your television is turned off to prevent television speaker damage. Then plug the jacks in, matching the color of the jack to the color of the input on your TV.

83

HARDWARE SETUP

Wii

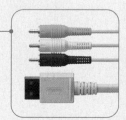
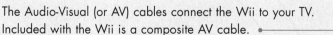

If your television is HD (High-Definition), three video jacks (red, green, and blue) and two audio jacks (red and white) should be on the back of your television. If this is the case, use a Wii Component Cable with five connectors to connect your Wii console unit to your television with better picture clarity. The Wii Component Cable is sold separately.

Plug the end of the AV cable with a large, single connector into the largest slot on the back of the Wii console unit. Align the connector to the slot properly so that the end of the cable with angled corners fits easily into the slot.

LIVING ROOM ARRANGEMENT

If you cannot stand on your feet for long, or simply prefer to play while seated, place a seat 4–15 feet from the television.

[TIP]
Avoid sitting or standing closer than three feet from the television to ensure proper controller signal and to avoid eyestrain. Fifteen feet is the maximum range at which the Wii Remote can send a motion signal to the sensor bar.

HARDWARE SETUP

84

[P O W E R   O n]

It's time to power up the Wii! First, turn on your television and make sure the channel is set to the proper input setting.

Then turn on the Wii console unit using one of three methods:

1. Press the power button on the face of the Wii console unit. The power button has an LED light that indicates the console's status:
   - A red light means that the system is idle.
   - A green light means that the system is on.
   - A yellow light means that the system is idle, but connected to the Internet via the WiiConnect24 options.

2. Press and hold the power button in the upper-left corner on the face of one Wii Remote controller until the Wii console unit turns on.

3. Insert a Wii or GameCube game disc into the self-loading disc slot. The console unit turns on when either a Wii or GameCube disc is inserted.

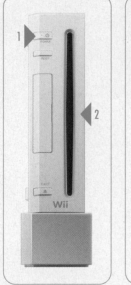

[NOTE]
THE GAME DISC SLOT
The game disc slot on the front of the console lights a blue color and blinks only when a game disc is inserted or when a new message has been received on the Wii Message Board. Do not be alarmed if it does not blink at other times!

[CAUTION]
INSERTING GAME DISCS CORRECTLY
If the console is placed vertically, the disc label should be facing the right when inserted. If the console is placed horizontally, insert the game disc with the disc label facing upward.

QUICK REFERENCE

85

POWER ON

[WII REMOTE CONTROL]

The Wii console unit comes packaged with one motion-sensitive Wii Remote controller.

- The Wii Remote requires two AA batteries.
- The Wii Remote works in unison with the sensor bar to read motions made with the Wii Remote.
- By moving the Wii Remote up or down, from left to right, or in any direction, the user can interact with the software being played and control the action.

QUICK REFERENCE

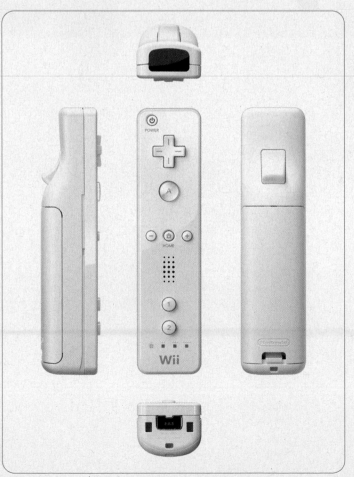

[TIP]
We strongly recommend purchasing rechargeable batteries for use with your Wii Remote(s).

86

Wii REMOTE

Wii REMOTE BUTTONS

The face of the Wii Remote features eight buttons that allow you to control games, applications, and the Wii System menu. A ninth button, the trigger-shaped Ⓑ, is on the underside of the Wii Remote.

- Power button ⏻
- 4-direction button ✛
- A button Ⓐ
- − button ⊖
- + button ⊕
- Home button ⌂
- 1 button ①
- 2 button ②
- B button Ⓑ

[N O T E]
Other features of the Wii Remote's face include a speaker that may emit sound effects while playing a game. The four blue lights near the base of the Wii Remote indicate which of the four wireless ports the controller is connected to.

If the first light (indicated with one dot above it) is lit, then it means that the Wii Remote is connected to player slot one, and the person using that controller will control the cursor hand marked "1" as well as the onscreen character designated as player one. Likewise, the remote connected to port two controls player character two, and so forth.

WIRELESS CONNECTION

The Wii Remote that comes with your Wii console unit should already be synced to connect wirelessly to your system. If the Wii is not responding to signals from the Wii Remote controller, first ensure that two AA batteries are inserted into the Wii Remote.

If the Wii Remote has power but the Wii console still does not respond to button presses, the Wii Remote may need to be synched with the console.

To sync the Wii Remote:

1. Open the battery cover. Press and release the small red button located below the batteries.
2. The player indicator lights near the bottom of the Wii Remote's face should all begin flashing.
3. Aim the Wii Remote at the front of the Wii console, then press and release the red button marked "sync" located on the front of the console under the SD memory card flap.
4. Wait until the Wii Remote connects to the console. When a blue player indicator light shines at the bottom of the Wii Remote, the connection is confirmed.

[N O T E]
If multiple players are to play, sync all Wii Remotes to the console one at a time depending on who wants to be player two, player three, and player four, in that order.

TEMPORARY SYNCH-UP

Take your Wii Remote to a friend's house to use your own controller to play on that system! To synch a remote to any Wii Console temporarily:

1. Press ⌂ on a Wii Remote already synched to the console to navigate to the Home menu.
2. Select the option at the bottom of the Home menu that says, "Wii Remote Settings."
3. Select the "Reconnect" button.
4. Press ① and ② simultaneously on the remote to temporarily connect. The LED lights on the controller should start blinking.
5. Wait for the console to establish a connection. When one blue LED light on the Wii Remote remains lit, the Wii Remote is then temporarily synched to play on the system until the console is turned off.

QUICK REFERENCE

87

WII REMOTE

WRIST STRAP

Whenever using the Wii Remote to control a game or to navigate system menus, always slip the wrist of your playing hand through the wrist strap. This helps prevent accidentally dropping or throwing the Wii Remote controller in the heat of action.

BASIC MENU NAVIGATION

The system menus of the Wii console as well as for several Wii games can be navigated simply by pointing the top of the Wii Remote toward the screen. The hand cursor onscreen indicates your pointing position. Point toward the desired menu choice or onscreen buttons and press Ⓐ to make a selection.

Point the remote at the screen and press Ⓐ to make menu selections. Hold the controller at whatever angle is most comfortable for your hand and wrist.

THE HOME BUTTON (⌂)

Whether you are playing a game, editing photos, or creating Mii characters, press ⌂ at any time to bring up the Home menu. This built-in function allows you to exit the game in-progress or active program and return to the main Wii Menu. You can also "Reset" the console to the startup screen.

Point at any of the "P1, P2, P3, P4" buttons at the bottom of the screen and press Ⓐ to configure the options for that controller, including:

- Changing the Wii Remote speaker volume.
- Turning rumble on or off.
- Reconnecting or one-time synching a Wii Remote to the console.

[N O T E]
The onscreen cursor has a number, indicating the player number as displayed on your Wii Remote control. Also, the hand cursor rotates as you rotate the controller!

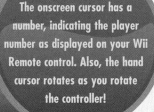

WII REMOTE

[The Nunchuck Controller]

If the game you're playing requires it, plug the Nunchuk attachment's cable into the expansion port slot on the bottom of the Wii Remote. The game typically displays some kind of warning screen if the Nunchuk is not attached and the game or program requires it.

The Nunchuk features a thumbstick control similar to the one on the GameCube controller. It also features ⓒ and ⓩ on the curved underside. The Nunchuk is motion sensitive like the Wii Remote, so moving it in the air while facing your television set should allow interaction with a game.

The Nunchuk cannot be used by itself; it only functions when plugged into the connector slot on the bottom of the Wii Remote controller. The Nunchuk controller has no functionality on any of the Wii system menus.

QUICK REFERENCE

89

NUNCHUCK

[NOTE]
AMBIDEXTROUS CONTROL

When using the Nunchuk in conjunction with the Wii Remote, hold the Wii Remote in your dominant hand. For instance, if you would play tennis with your right hand, then you should also hold the Wii Remote with your right hand. If you would play left-handed, then hold the Wii Remote in your left hand. When playing a two-handed game such as the Boxing mode of *Wii Sports*, hold the Wii Remote in your right hand and hold the Nunchuk in your left hand if you are right handed. If not, then switch the controllers around so that the Wii Remote is in your left hand.

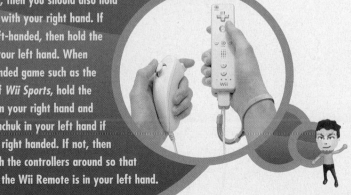

[GAMECUBE CONTROLLER AND MEMORY CARD PORTS]

On the left side of the Wii console unit (or on the top, if your Wii is placed on the vertical stand) are two flip lids. Underneath the longer flip lid are four GameCube controller ports. Two GameCube memory card ports are under the smaller flip lid.

If you wish to play GameCube games on the Wii, connect GameCube controllers or Wavebird wireless controllers to one or more of these ports. To save your progress in a GameCube game, you must insert a GameCube memory card into one of the two memory card ports. Connect GameCube controllers and memory cards to the Wii before inserting an 8.5cm GameCube disc into the self-loading drive to ensure proper game startup and operation.

[CAUTION]
To play GameCube software on the Wii, you must use GameCube controllers and memory cards. The Wii Remote, Nunchuk, and Wii Classic controllers are not compatible with GameCube games. You cannot save your progress from a GameCube game to the flash memory or to an SD memory card; GameCube game data can be saved only to a GameCube memory card.

[TIP]
If your console is lying horizontally, remove the flip lids covering the GameCube controller and memory card ports so that the unit remains lying flat when the lids are open. The flip lids snap right off and easily snap back on.

GAMECUBE

[WII SYSTEM CONFIGURATION]

Upon starting your Wii console for the first time, you must determine basic settings for the system. After you've selected choices for the system, you can change these settings at any time by entering the Wii Settings menu using the option in the bottom-left corner of the Wii Channel menu.

1. Select your preferred language: English, Français, or Español.
2. Indicate the sensor bar's position (Above TV, Below TV).
3. Set the date.
4. Set the time in military (24 hour) time. For instance, 2:45 in afternoon would be 14:45 and 8:30 PM would be 20:30.
5. Set the screen resolution (standard 4:3 or widescreen 16:9).
6. Choose a console nickname. Point the Wii Remote's cursor at the white bar onscreen and press Ⓐ to enter the Wii virtual keyboard. Type in a nickname for console (up to 10 characters) by pointing at letters and pressing Ⓐ. Choose the "CAPS" button to type in all capital letters, or choose the "Shift" button to make only your next letter capitalized.
7. Choose whether or not to use parental controls. If you chose to, enter a password. With the parental controls enabled, if the game is rated M for Mature by the ESRB (Entertainment Software Ratings Board, more info at *www.esrb.com*), then the game cannot be played until a parent or adult enters the password. (Not applicable to GameCube games.)

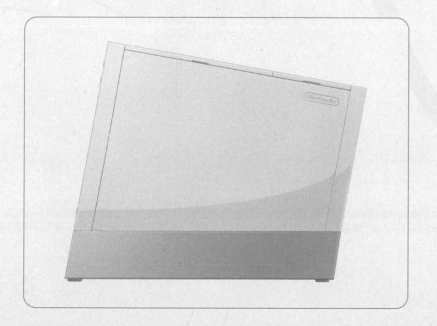

QUICK REFERENCE

91

WII SYSTEM
CONFIGURATION

You and Wii™

QUICK REFERENCE

[WII MENU]

The Wii Menu is the main operation menu of the Wii console unit. Each time the Wii is turned on, the console boots to a black screen. Press Ⓐ on any Wii Remote connected wirelessly to the system to continue to the Wii Menu.

Programs available on the Wii Menu are presented as small television screens called "channels." To activate a channel, point the Wii Remote at the channel and press Ⓐ on the Wii Remote.

When a channel is selected, that channel takes over the screen. Cycle through the available channels by pressing ⊖ and ⊕ on the Wii Remote.

When the desired channel takes over the screen, move the hand cursor down to the buttons near the bottom of the display. Select "Wii Menu" to return to the main screen, or select "Start" to use the displayed program.

Notice two more options near the bottom of the Wii Menu: The button in the screen's bottom-left corner opens the Wii Options menu. The button in the bottom-right corner opens the Wii Message Board. We shall focus on these two functions for now and save the channel functions for later.

[W i i   O p t i o n s]

Notice the small circle marked "Wii" in the lower-left corner of the Wii Menu. Use the Wii Remote controller to point at this circle, and press Ⓐ to select it. This action opens the Wii Options menu.

The first screen displays three options. "Data Management" allows you to view saved games stored on either the 512MB flash memory incorporated into the Wii, or GameCube saves stored on a GameCube memory card inserted into one of the two memory card slots. "Wii Settings" lets you view and make changes to the system configuration options. The "Back" button at the bottom of the screen returns you to the Wii Menu.

QUICK REFERENCE

93

Wii OPTIONS

You and Wii™

[DATA MANAGEMENT]

Select the "Data Management" option to view and manage game saves. In the sub-menu, choose whether to view save data stored on memory devices attached to the Wii, or to view channels saved to your memory.

SAVE DATA

Choosing this option opens a sub-screen. Choose whether to view Wii save data or GameCube saves.

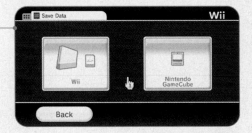

Wii DATA

Save game data from Wii games and Virtual Console games are initially saved to the onboard 512M flash memory and displayed in the Wii data sub-menu. Use this menu to copy saved games to an SD memory card inserted into the SD card slot on the front of the Wii console.

Use the Wii Remote to point at a save, and press Ⓐ to select it. Use the pop-up menu to "erase" the save or "copy" it to an SD memory card.

DATA MANAGEMENT

[TIP]
The flash memory inside the Wii allows you to store up to 2,163 blocks of data, including saved games, Virtual Console games, and channel data. To determine how many blocks of data a game requires to create a save, check the back of the game box.

94

NINTENDO GAMECUBE DATA

Insert a GameCube memory card into the first or second slot on the side of the Wii console unit. If your Wii is placed in the vertical stand, the memory card slot is on the top of the unit. Insert the card into "Slot A" or "Slot B," as marked.

After inserting a Nintendo GameCube card into one of the available slots, enter the Data Management menu and choose the "Nintendo GameCube" option. Any GameCube save games stored on the memory card are displayed onscreen.

Use the Wii Remote control to highlight a GameCube saved game, and press Ⓐ to view the statistics and date of the saved game and also open a pop-up menu full of choices. GameCube saved games can be erased or copied to another memory card inserted into the other slot.

[CAUTION]
GameCube saved games cannot be copied to any other storage format: not the flash memory, and not an SD memory card.

QUICK REFERENCE

95

DATA MANAGEMENT

CHANNELS

The Channels sub-menu allows you to view downloaded channel data, such as Virtual Console games. Amazingly, an entire game such as Super Mario 64 takes up only 90 blocks on your Wii flash memory!

Select a channel data in the Channels menu to bring up a pop-up menu that allows you to "copy" downloaded channels to an SD memory card inserted into the SD card slot on the front of the Wii console, or to "erase" downloaded data.

[CAUTION]
Copying channel data to a portable storage device such as an SD memory card is a great idea. But note that you cannot transfer channel data such as Virtual Console games from one console to another; the downloaded games will not play on any console except the one they were originally downloaded to.

[TIP]
Virtual Console games downloaded from the Wii Shop Channel can be downloaded again at any time for free. So if you accidentally delete a game from the Channels menu, don't sweat it!

QUICK REFERENCE

DATA MANAGEMENT

[WII SETTINGS]

Choose the "Wii Settings" option to change the console's configuration. The Wii System Settings menu is divided into three pages. Point at the arrow on the screen's right and press Ⓐ to advance to the next page of options. Point at the "Back" button and press Ⓐ if you want to return to the Wii System menu. The following text details the options available on the three System Settings pages.

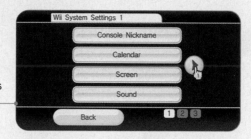

CONSOLE NICKNAME

Choose this option to change your console's name. On the sub-screen, point at the white box in the center and press Ⓐ to bring up a virtual keyboard.

On the virtual keyboard, use the Wii Remote to point at the desired letters and press Ⓐ to type. To cancel entering a new name and go back to the previous screen, choose the "Quit" option in the screen's lower left. Choose "OK" in the screen's lower right to confirm the name change.

CALENDAR

This option allows you to change the date and time on the Wii. Point the Wii Remote at either option and press Ⓐ to change the value.

The date is in month/day/year format. To increase any number, use the Wii Remote to point at the arrows above the number and press Ⓐ. To decrease any number, move the hand cursor to the arrows below any number and press Ⓐ.

WII SETTINGS

97

The time is in 24-hour time format, also known as "military time." Thus, 00:00 is midnight and 12:00 is noon. Any time between midnight and noon may be entered as is. For instance, 8:45 AM can simply be entered as 08:45. Any time between noon and midnight must be entered as a number between 12:00 and 23:59. For instance, 2:15 PM must be entered as 14:15.

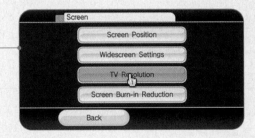

[TIP]
Understanding Military Time
The key to understanding military time is to take any time in the afternoon and add 12:00. Thus, 5:30 becomes 17:30, 7:05 becomes 19:05, and so forth.

SCREEN

Choose the "Screen" option to change the way the Wii System menu and games are displayed onscreen. The Screen sub-menu has four options:

Screen Position: If a black line is visible on either side of the screen, or if a portion of the screen seems to be falling off the side, then you should change the screen position. Point the Wii Remote at the arrows to the left and right of the central number and press Ⓐ to adjust the screen position. When the display looks acceptable, point at the "Confirm" button and press Ⓐ to return to the previous menu.

Widescreen Settings: Choose the ratio of display to match your television screen size. "Standard (4:3)" is the format of standard tube televisions with composite cable input. "Widescreen (16:9)" is the better choice for widescreen projection, plasma, or LCD televisions with HD quality component video input connectors.

TV Resolution: Use this option to change the picture quality. "EDTV or HDTV (480p)" is available only for HD-ready widescreen televisions. If your Wii is connected to your television through the composite cable, then this option is grayed out. "Standard TV (480i)" is the resolution of a standard tube television. The Wii's image quality is significantly sharper and improved when viewed on an EDTV or HDTV through a component cable connection.

Screen Burn-in Reduction: Choose whether to turn burn-in reduction "On" or "Off." If the Wii is connected to a widescreen projection, LCD, or plasma screen television, we strongly recommend turning this option on. When enabled, the screen goes several shades darker if left idle for more than a few minutes. This helps to prevent the image from burning onto the screen permanently and ruining your television.

SOUND

Choose the sound setting that is appropriate for your television or home configuration. Typically, most televisions nowadays are equipped with "Stereo" sound speakers, making this the best option to choose for most homes. "Mono" sound may be a good option to choose if one of the speakers on your television is broken.

If your television is connected to a home theater surround sound system, then the absolute best option to choose is "Surround" sound. Be sure to turn on your home theater system to enable the best sound quality in this mode.

[CAUTION]
Remember that video games play much louder than cable television or DVDs, so compensate by turning down the volume slightly to avoid hearing damage or neighbor annoyance.

PARENTAL CONTROLS

Enable parental controls to block young children from playing games rated "M" for Mature by the Entertainment Software Ratings Board (ESRB) without the permission of an adult. Point the Wii Remote at the "Yes" option on the Parental Controls sub-screen and press Ⓐ to go to the next screen. An adult must set a 4-digit pin number password to lock out M-rated games. Set the password when the child is not in the room. Once this option is set, "M" rated games cannot be played on the Wii unless the password is correctly entered.

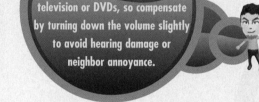

As the warning on the Parental Controls sub-screen indicates, this function does not block the playing of M-rated Nintendo GameCube games.

[CAUTION]
If you are a parent and do not wish your child to play an M-rated GameCube game, then place those games out of the child's reach. Or, prevent the child from using the Wii entirely while left alone or in the care of a babysitter. One effective way to prevent a child from playing games without adult supervision is to remove the power cable from the Wii and take the cable with you when you are not at home.

[TIP]
Setting the Parental Controls also prevents children from messing with Internet connection options and disallows purchase or download of Virtual Console games from the Wii Shop Channel without parental permission, in the form of the 4-digit pin.

QUICK REFERENCE

99

WII SETTINGS

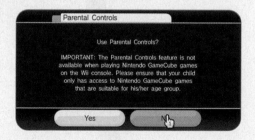

WII SETTINGS

SENSOR BAR

To better facilitate the motion sensor functionality of the Wii Remotes and sensor bar, enter the Sensor Bar sub-screen in the Wii System Settings menu. Use the Wii Remote to point at either "Sensor Bar Position" or "Sensitivity" and press Ⓐ to confirm your choice.

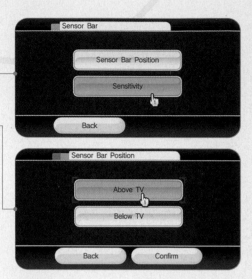

Change the "Sensor Bar Position" option based on where your sensor bar is placed in relation to your television set:

- If you intend to sit while playing, then placing the sensor bar below the TV pointed at your sitting position should provide the best Wii Remote motion sensitivity.
- If you stand while playing the game, then place the sensor bar above the TV and change your settings to suit the device's location.

While playing a game or browsing the Wii channels, change the Sensitivity setting if you feel that the Wii is not responding well enough to motions made with the Wii Remote:

1. Point the Wii Remote at the "OK" button to bypass the warning messages and proceed to the Sensitivity Setting screen.
2. Point the Wii at the center of the screen and notice two white dots indicating where the Wii Remote is pointing.
3. Move the Wii Remote to move the two dots inside the gray center area.
4. If the two dots are moving too slowly or too quickly for your control, then press the ⊖ or ⊕ buttons to decrease or increase the system's sensitivity to the motion of the Wii Remote.

INTERNET

The Internet sub-screens allow you to connect the Wii to a wireless Internet router, to a USB Internet connection, or to a Nintendo Wi-Fi USB Connector.

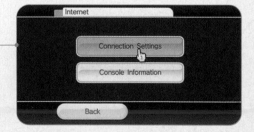

CONNECTION SETTINGS

Choose the first option on the Internet sub-screen to configure the type of Internet connection for the Wii. Up to three connection profiles may be stored in the Wii's memory. When the console is turned on, it automatically connects to the Internet using these settings.

After selecting a connection to configure, choose whether the connection will be a Wireless Connection or a Wired Connection.

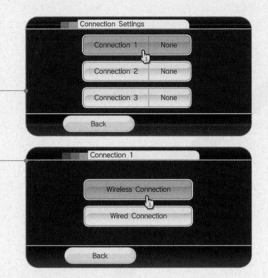

CONNECTING TO A WIRELESS NETWORK ACCESS POINT

To configure a wireless connection, you must have already fulfilled the following requirements:

1. Subscribed to broadband Internet service through a DSL or cable modem provider.
2. Connected a high-speed modem and wireless router to the broadband adapter installed in your home by your Internet provider.
3. Configured your wireless router or hub for either a secured or unsecured network. For the safety of your home computers, personal data, and your Nintendo Wii, we strongly recommend configuring your wireless router or hub with some form of encryption, such as WEP or WPA. This mainly prevents outside users from leeching off your Internet connection, which can slow your data transmission speed. See the instructions included with the wireless access point for more information.
4. Configured the settings of your wireless access point to enable connections by all types of wireless devices, not just those made by the same manufacturer. See the instructions included with the wireless access point for more information.
5. Or, instead of the aforementioned steps, you must have installed and connected a Nintendo Wi-Fi USB Connector to a PC that is connected to the Internet via a broadband cable.

After selecting the Wireless Connection option, choose whether to "Search for an Access Point," connect to a "Nintendo Wi-Fi USB Connector," or to configure a "Manual Setup."

Choose the "Search for an Access Point" option if a wireless network is set up in your home. The Nintendo Wii spends a few seconds searching for wireless Internet access points within range. When the Wii is finished searching, all access points within range are displayed.

QUICK REFERENCE

WII SETTINGS

For each available wireless access point, the Wii displays the name of the connection, whether the connection is secured by encryption or not, and the strength of the signal. A wireless access point inside your home should have excellent signal strength. Access points outside the home should have very weak signals. Therefore, if you accidentally configured your wireless access point with the same name as your neighbor's you should be able to tell the difference by signal strength.

If the access point's signal is secured, then the Wii prompts you to enter the password or key. Your wireless access point should have created this password or numbered key while you were configuring it for a secure signal in your home. If you do not remember the password or encryption key, consult the instruction manual of your wireless access point to determine how to use a PC to retrieve that data.

Should the connection test prove successful, the system then prompts you to check the Internet for Wii system updates. Select "OK" to check for updates. Updating the system allows you to keep your Wii system ready for new channels, new configurations, and the requirements of new games.

Whether an update is available or not, the system reboots and returns to the Wii Menu channel screen.

Wii SETTINGS

Connecting to a Nintendo Wi-Fi USB Connector

If you have installed a Nintendo Wi-Fi USB Connector to a Windows XP PC in your home that is connected to the broadband Internet, then simply choose the option "Nintendo Wi-Fi USB Connector." The Wii sends a signal to the connector attached to your PC. Return to your PC and click on the Wi-Fi Registration Tool icon on your desktop system tray. Your Nintendo Wii's nickname should appear with a small yellow "?" next to it. Click on the Wii's nickname and select "Grant permission to connect."

The Wii is then connected wirelessly to the Internet through your wired PC. The PC must be on and connected to the Internet for the Wii to connect to the Internet.

Connecting to a Wired (USB) Connection

To configure a wired connection, you must have completed the following steps prior to powering on the Wii:

1. Subscribed to broadband service through a DSL or cable modem provider.
2. Purchased the Wii USB Internet modem sold separately and connected it into one of the USB slots on the backside of the console.
3. Connected a high-speed modem and Internet hub or router with USB connection ports to the broadband adapter installed in your home by your Internet provider.
4. Connected the Wii USB Internet modem to the USB access point via a USB cable.

[NOTE]
Note that with a wired connection, your home entertainment system and Nintendo Wii must be placed very close to the USB Internet hub in your home. With a wireless connection, the Wii can connect to the Internet from another room in your house.

Manual Setup

Manual connections are extremely tricky. Thanks to the simplicity of most wired and wireless Internet technology, there should be almost no reason to use this option unless you are having trouble connecting the Wii to an Internet connection in your home. We strongly recommend contacting Nintendo technical support for help with Manual Setup of an Internet connection. You may contact Nintendo through their website at *www.nintendo.com* or by calling Nintendo support at **1-800-895-1672**.

QUICK REFERENCE

103

CONNECTION OPTIONS

After successfully creating an Internet connection, the Nintendo Wii saves your settings. The next time you choose a connection that has already been established, a new menu of options appears:

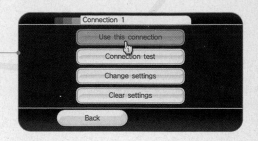

Use this connection: If more than one connection type has been established, select this option to make the Wii connect to the chosen connection every time the power is turned on.

Connection test: If you are not sure whether the Wii is properly connected to the Internet through this connection, choose this option. After several seconds of testing, a message appears indicating whether the connection is valid or not.

Change settings: If the settings were configured manually and do not appear to be working, choose this option to return to the Manual Setup sub-screens.

Clear settings: Deletes all settings and disconnects from the connection source. Use this option if you wish to start from scratch.

CONSOLE INFORMATION

The second option on the Internet sub-screen allows you to view the MAC address of the Wii console as well as any USB Ethernet Adapter that may be connected to the unit. These numbers may be needed if you must grant access for the console to connect to your wired connection.

USER AGREEMENTS

This option appears only after your system is updated or additional channels are downloaded, such as the Wii Shop Channel. Select this option only if you wish to re-read the user agreement for the Wii Shop Channel or other channels and agree or disagree with the statement.

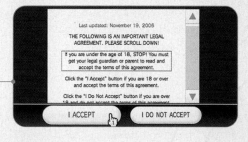

QUICK REFERENCE

104

WiiCONNECT24

The Wii console can communicate with the Internet even when the power is turned off. The WiiConnect24 service delivers system updates, game updates, messages from friends, or other surprises even if the system is idle. The sub-menu provides three options:

WiiConnect24: Choose whether the WiiConnect24 option remains on or off. If off, the other options remain grayed out.

Standby Connection: Choose whether the standby connection option is on or off. This is the basic component of WiiConnect24. When the console is powered off but remains plugged into an electrical outlet, the LED indicator on the power button turns yellow to indicate that the system is monitoring the Internet for new messages and updates.

Slot Illumination: Choose how brightly the slot illuminates when a new message is received via the Internet, or set the option to "OFF." The slot illumination could prove annoying if the Wii is located in your bedroom and lights up while you are sleeping. Change this setting to prevent losing rest!

LANGUAGE

The various Wii menus can be displayed on North American consoles in three languages: English, French, or Spanish. If you choose a new language, the Wii console must reboot.

COUNTRY

Select your country of residence to enable faster downloading through the Internet and other benefits of localization.

QUICK REFERENCE

105

QUICK REFERENCE

WII SYSTEM UPDATE

This option connects the Wii to the Internet to perform a Wii system update and keep your console ready for the newest channels and features available. The system reboots after completing a check for system updates, download, and installation.

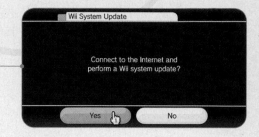

FORMAT WII SYSTEM MEMORY

Choose this option to clear the flash memory and restore the Wii console system to its factory default settings. When the format is finished and the console reboots, you must reset the initial options.

[CAUTION]
Formatting the flash memory drive wipes out all game saves as well as all photos or videos stored on the Wii Message Board. So make sure not to erase your game's progress or delete your characters if that is not your desire. This function also deletes any new channels you may have downloaded as well as any Virtual Console games obtained. These items can be downloaded again once you have reconfigured your system and logged in. Formatting the flash memory does not affect data stored on GameCube memory cards or on SD memory cards inserted into the console at the time.

WII SETTINGS

[WII MESSAGE BOARD]

In the lower-right corner of the Wii Menu is a small circular button with an envelope symbol. Point at this button with the Wii Remote and press Ⓐ to enter the Wii Message Board, where you and your family can post memos to one another, view Today's Accomplishments lists, and view photos or videos posted to the message board through Photo Channel.

To view accomplishments and messages from other days, point the Wii Remote at the arrows on the sides of the screen and press Ⓐ to switch to another date, or press ⊖ or ⊕. The Calendar menu in the screen's bottom-left corner allows you to view messages from previous days and earlier months.

[TIP]
If a small number flashes beneath the envelope symbol on the Wii Menu, new items have been posted to the message board since the last viewing.

TODAY'S ACCOMPLISHMENTS

The amount of time spent playing games or working in Mii Channel, Photo Channel, Wii Shop Channel, or other channels is logged in a message that is posted to the message board. This allows parents or others to view what activities have been taking place on the console all day, if any. Today's Accomplishments cannot be trashed.

[TIP]
Press up or down on ✛ to scroll through Today's Accomplishments. You may also highlight the arrows at the top or bottom of the screen and press Ⓐ to scroll.

QUICK REFERENCE

107

Wii MESSAGE BOARD

QUICK REFERENCE

CALENDAR

The calendar allows you to view at a glance which days had activity on the console. Any date with activity or messages is marked with a small envelope. Today's date is highlighted in yellow.

To jump to another month, press ⊖ or ⊕, or point at the arrows on the side of the screen and press Ⓐ. To jump to a specific date, point the hand cursor at the date and press Ⓐ to view messages received and activities performed on that day.

CREATE MESSAGE

You can post memos and photos for friends and family members on the Wii Message Board. You can also send e-mails and photos to friends via an Internet connection. Choose the "Create Message" button in the bottom-left corner of the screen to create any kind of message.

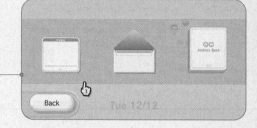

POSTING MEMOS

Select the first option on the left side of the screen if you wish to post a memo to a friend or family member who also uses the Wii during the day. You may want to remind your brother or sister not to over-write your *Legend of Zelda: Twilight Princess* game save, or maybe you just need to remind someone to get some potatoes at the store.

- Click the box next to "Add a Mii" to add your Mii likeness to the memo, or to add the likeness of a friend or family member so that they understand who the message is for.
- Click in the "Write a memo" area and use the virtual keyboard to compose a message.

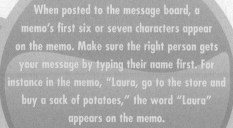

[TIP]

When posted to the message board, a memo's first six or seven characters appear on the memo. Make sure the right person gets your message by typing their name first. For instance in the memo, "Laura, go to the store and buy a sack of potatoes," the word "Laura" appears on the memo.

WII MESSAGE BOARD

108

VIEWING MEMOS

When a memo is posted to the message board, it appears as a small sticky note. Highlight it with the hand cursor and press Ⓐ to view it.

To erase a memo, point at the small trash can button in the screen's upper left and press Ⓐ to erase the message. After you confirm erasure, the message is permanently removed from the message board.

SEND A MESSAGE

On the Create Message sub-screen, select the yellow envelope in the center to compose a message to be transmitted through the Internet.

Upon selecting this option, the address book appears. You must add people to your address book before you can send them messages. To send a message to a person, highlight his or her nickname in the address book and press Ⓐ. You can send messages to other Wii consoles or e-mail addresses.

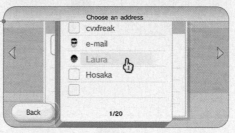

- Writing a message is like writing a memo; simply click in the "Write a message" area to bring up the virtual keyboard and compose your message.
- Add a Mii character to your message by clicking in the small square in the message's upper-left corner. E-mail recipients will not receive a Mii character.

ADDRESS BOOK

Choose the third option on the Create Message sub-screen to add e-mail addresses and other Wii consoles to your address book. Click the "Register" button to add a message recipient to your address book.

QUICK REFERENCE

109

Wii MESSAGE BOARD

On the registration sub-screen, choose whether the recipient is another Wii console or an e-mail address.

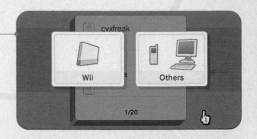

REGISTRATION TYPES

If the recipient is another Wii console, you must register that console by exchanging your console's 16 digit Wii Number with that person. View your Wii Number by pressing ⊖ to go to the first page of your address book. Both persons must register each other's Wii Numbers before messages can be exchanged through your Wii consoles.

If the recipient is a person on a computer or cellular phone, you must register that person by entering his or her e-mail address. An e-mail with registration information will be sent to that person, and he or she must agree to the terms of service before e-mails can be exchanged.

110

WII MESSAGE BOARD